For Mum

As
Found

*(definition: in an imperfect state;
distressed through the passage of time)*

By

Michael Baggott

Chapters

Chapter 1: Epiphany in Stoke

Everything has to begin somewhere.

Over the years it's been assumed I either come from a lineage of venerable antiques dealers (sharing my surname with a family of dealers from Stow in the Wold) or I'm the wealthy dilettante bastard offspring of a minor errant noble. Nothing, nothing could be further from the truth.

Castle Vale was a tower blocked, burning car, demilitarised zone in Birmingham. Not the half way pretty (if it was ever that) Victorian Industrial heart of Birmingham, but the vast sprawling suburban spaghetti of roads and roundabouts. Broken, abandoned, falling down factories rubbed shoulders with rows of faded terraces which surrounded and encompassed them, a disused and neglected canal snaked through them all. This was my playground, this was where I grew up.

Childhood summer holidays were long, too long, six weeks long, with nothing to do. As a boy there was no television until the early afternoon so you played in the street or the garden, or indoors with hours of cards, draughts and chess.

Day trips were the only highlights of these holidays.

Dad worked early mornings down the wholesale market and slept in most of the day, Granddad did the same, though his state of inactivity and horizontal position were less to do with odd working times than with a life's ambition to sleep and gamble in equal measure. The women, the matriarchs in our family did EVERYTHING. I was constantly to be found in the company of both my Nan and my Mum.

Nan was a small unassuming lady. When out always immaculately dressed. Loving, caring and fair minded, though with a strict set of rules you would only infringe on at your peril. Rarely a boorish man might mistake Nan for a frail old lady only to discover, to his regret, that she was in fact harder than a coffin nail. Woe betide the person in front of her at a checkout that lapsed into friendly conversation with the cashier holding up the queue. She had made Spitfires during the War and that, believe me, was why we had won.

My Mum was not at all like Nan, and I was made for the most part just like her. Shy, kind (much kinder than me) and funny, she would always have walked away rather than fought, from tip to toe she was full of love and a ceaseless ability to work AND she was the only person in the family who could drive, so the lynch pin not just of her children's hearts but of every Summer day trip.

They both loved flowers and gardening and had seen on the evening's regional news that Stoke on Trent council were holding a "Garden Festival", so we were all going to go for a day out, wether I liked it or not.

The following morning we were bundled into the car, I sat in the back to look after that morning's buttered and cling filmed cheese and tomato sandwiches and a thermos of sweet tea in a carrier bag (no one ever thought to pay to eat out on our day trips). We buckled up and drove for what seemed like ages until we arrived at Trentham Gardens in Stoke on Trent, where the festival was being held.

It was like a very floral amusement park when we arrived, but with fewer rides. There was a map of the festival showing you all the exotically named areas, pathways and where all the "activities" were. Perhaps a hastily erected merry-go-round themed around Geraniums, or a slide covered with Roses, the thorns pricking toddlers legs as they slid down. The sun shone and we all walked and walked and walked, admiring one spectacular municipal floral display after another.

After several hours there was a reprieve, legs were getting tired and we could go and sit down near the "Etruria" area of the festival where all the good potters of Stoke had gathered to off load their factory seconds to unsuspecting tourists.

You might think this nearly as uninteresting as looking at flowers to a boy almost in his teens, but my Nan had taken me with her to every January sale in one of the then big department stores (Beatties) since I could remember. This was where she would buy Wedgwood or Derby porcelain at cut throat prices.

Cut throat was right. I think the starkly competitive nature of it, middle aged well dressed women jostling, elbowing you in the chest then stamping on your feet, to get a substantially reduced twelve plate Coalport set of the "Days of Christmas" had meant I'd got swept up with it, well, with the thrill of the hunt at least. On my shelf at home, alongside my Star Wars sticker book, set of Tintin novels and Lego were one or two small, boxed (never take them out of the box) Wedgwood trinkets, which had been bought at greatly reduced prices.

"Can I stay here and look around Nan?" I asked, now completely "flowered-out"

She nodded and I was briefly allowed to run around the square pavilion of stalls. First I did the inside stands, there was nothing I liked. Though Mum did buy an enormous decorated Meat Platter for £3 which for the next twenty years was to become my Dad's Sunday dinner plate, piled high with enough roast meat, Yorkshire pudding and potatoes to feed the five thousand. Nan and Mum then sat down as I quickly ran around the outside stalls.

All the hustle and bustle had been inside, the layout wasn't great and the outside perimeter of small booths had a church like quiet. I ran around the edge, "plates, plates, more plates", well it was Stoke, the heart of the potteries. Then I stopped dead in my tracks, just as if an invisible wall had leapt up and hit me. I turned slowly and approached the small booth just beside me.

A large, seemingly huge, dark wooden glazed display case formed the entire front of the booth. It had several shelves lined with dark, perhaps black or was it blue velvet? Unaware of myself and of any of the attendant shyness I usually displayed, I placed both hands, palm open, on the glass and lent in, pressing my face to nearly touch the contents.

I will never know why, to this day, the wonderful, patient antiques dealer whose booth this was had determined to come to the Stoke on Trent Garden Festival, but thank God she did.

She had come with every manner of antique silver object you can imagine, vesta cases, vinaigrettes, spoons, fruit knives, wine labels, card cases, thimbles, pepperettes, chatelaines, forks, novelties, everything you could possibly imagine was there. I had never really seen antiques before, not in real life, not "in the wild" and the experience was both intoxicating and overwhelming. I was immediately enchanted by the glittering treasures that lay before me. This was my Howard Carter moment, all I could see were "wonderful things"

The stall holder was not busy, there was nobody around so (I suspect out of boredom and kindness to a small boy) she began to show me pieces from out of the cases, though I couldn't quite believe I actually got to hold them.

After a good while I ran back to fetch my Mum as she held the purse strings. There was a knife (I was not so much a small boy that I didn't like the idea of a knife) with a solid silver handle and it was nearly two hundred years old, "come and see". I ran, pulling Mum back to the stand and asked if I might have the £22 to buy the knife out of my savings. At £3 pocket money a week this was a substantial sum of money and she was wary, so sensibly, but sadly, we left without it. Still the damage had been done, the antiques bug had bitten me, bitten hard.

Childhood fads come and go, I'd had a few up to that point (lead soldiers, stamps, brass rubbing etc) but I was unrelenting in my pursuit of an antiques shop.

Pestering my poor Mum, when we'd got home from Stoke, in that insistent annoying way children are best at, "Mum, Mum, Mum…" After a week of it and with no sign of me letting up we went into town to do our weekend shopping but found, for the first time (before then we had never looked), no less than THREE local antiques shops.

We took the Goldilocks approach, one was very, very upmarket selling furniture and paintings to local wealthy businessmen (too hot), one was full of porcelain and nick-nacks and overseen by a stern old woman (too cold), the last was run by an impish but kindly old man who walked with a stick and it almost exclusively stocked and sold antique silver (just right). This was the one that was to prove a second home for my remaining childhood years.

It is rare to look back on your life and point to the very day, to the very moment which would shape the rest of it. My "Epiphany in Stoke" was one such perfect day. Surrounded by the people I loved most in the World, with the entire future and path of my life being decided by a single chance encounter, even though I did not realise it at the time.

Chapter 2: Saturdays with Parry

Today the world is a much simpler place than when I was a boy. Simpler in that you can type a keyword into any number of search engines or social media apps and be instantly taken to a wealth of information on any subject and a community of people who share your particular interest. Things back in the early 80's just weren't that simple.

It was the end of a hot 80's summer and a week earlier, as a family, we had all gone to a garden festival in Stoke. By happenstance and misadventure I had, for the first time in my life, seen antiques, real genuine honest to goodness antiques. I'd handled all manner of small silver objects but sensibly, my Mum and Nan had viewed the whole thing with suspicion and mistrust (which was to persist for many more years to come), so I was not allowed to spend a single penny of my saved up pocket money on a Georgian silver handled table knife. It all stayed in my pocket and accompanied me back home, though along with it was a growing desire to own my very first antique.

By the second week of persistent parental nagging, following my "epiphany in Stoke", any hope that this might be a passing fad of mine had waned and familial resistance was at a low ebb, their defences had been worn down. If only they had remained firm I could now be an accomplished Surgeon, famous Barrister or a wealthy Banker rather than a humble penniless totter.

The world of antiques was simply a foreign land to a working class family from Birmingham and no one had the first clue where to start.

The door to the cupboard under the stairs was opened. It was where we kept thick coats, Wellingtons and the vacuum cleaner. In the corner was a thin plywood shelf supporting that year's copy of the Yellow Pages which was quickly retrieved and then flicked through to "A" for "antiques".

My Mum and Nan, though still deeply suspicious and disapproving of the enterprise, looked through the directory and to their great surprise found a short list of local antiques shops, a list they would never have looked for in a million years were it not for their peculiar little charge.

There were three antique shops all close by to the shopping centre we always visited at the weekend. The plan was "Operation Goldilocks". We would visit all three after the shopping was done, that following

Saturday. Mum would take me to each one in turn and be there just in case her young son did something incredibly stupid.

Excitement and a little fear (I was always painfully shy) welled up at the prospect of visiting the three shops the following weekend. First the weekly shopping had to be done, the familiar two to three hour marathon of WHSmith, Woolworths, Boots, The Indoor Market, Beatties, BHS and M&S. Then attention turned to the antiques shops which lined the old high street going up the hill from the Shopping Centre.

The first was what you might all imagine an antiques shop to be if you'd never been in one before. Victorian clutter, glass, brass and china all presided over by a "refined" white haired old lady, sitting in a chair like a spider in the centre of a web. In the best tradition of the Dickensian novel this character from central casting had no time for children, or the working class, so a working class child was clearly rubbing salt into the wound. Mum and I left almost as quickly as we had entered, stepping out into the late morning air which felt much warmer than the reception we had just received.

The other two shops were on opposite sides of the road to one another, further up at the top of the hill.

As the road was a busy main one we decided not to cross but continue up to where we could look at the second shop and then use the Pelican crossing to get to the third.

The second shop we did not even dare to enter. As we approached we could see it was a whole period house with large glazed bay windows displaying sumptuous and ornate Georgian furniture with four and five figure price tags, with lavish oils hanging in gilt frames behind that. "Thomas Coulbourn & Sons" was the shop where a stockbroker would blow his bonus, not a schoolboy spend his pocket money, so all our dwindling hopes were now firmly pinned on the one shop that remained.

Facing this lavish premises was the Odeon cinema, which Mum had taken me to innumerable times, though I had never before noticed the small shop just to the left of it, a small inconspicuous shop, sandwiched between the cinema and a branch of the then Midland Bank, simply called "H & R.L.Parry".

The shop was small and on one floor. It had large single pane windows either side of a central door which allowed you to see the whole shop at once. To the left was a low display counter and then an upright display case. In the middle, set back a little, was a large oak leather inset desk and matching armchair. The right hand side of the shop had another slim display case and then space for a handful of pieces of furniture. All the cases were full of small silver and the left hand shop window was a cream lined velvet shelf, strewn with all manner of antique silver knick-knackery.

I was just tall enough to rest my arms on the low outside ledge of the window and press my face up against the glass, transfixed and peering. Nothing there would elicit the slightest spark of interest from me now, but then, then it was like I had stumbled across Aladdin's cave brimming with treasure and my gaze was wide eyed and fixed.

"Come on then" my Mum said as she ushered me towards the door. Painfully shy or not, I was going in.

As the door opened a Victorian brass shop bell mounted on a coiled steel spring, fitted above it, let out a shrill ring and I then heard heavy, irregular footsteps, on creaking stairs as a figure appeared through a side door. This was the proprietor, Mr Parry who lived with his wife in the flat above.

Even then, when I first met him, Mr Parry looked as old as Methuselah. Short and round with a loose short sleeved shirt, smart pressed trousers and a signet ring on his finger, yellow butter gold, gypsy set with a frankly enormous diamond which flashed and sparkled with all the colours of the rainbow as he slightly limped and shuffled into the shop. He imparted welcome even before saying anything, thanks to his broad grin and smiling eyes glinting from behind his bloodhound jowls.

"What can I do for you young man?"

I froze and it was for my Mum to save the day

"He'd like to look at some of the boxes in the window" she said holding my hand and pulling me forward towards the counter "but he doesn't know anything" she very sensibly added.

Mr Parry gave me a glancing, calming smile as he shuffled over to the window and reached out a selection of six or seven horn and steel nineteenth century snuff boxes. He pulled a rectangular velvet lined tray from beneath the counter and started to arrange them in front of me. I noticed the various small white card price tags, on one side "c.1820 or c.1840" was written and on the other the prices ranging from £18-28.

Gingerly, nervously, like I was about to diffuse a 1000lb unexploded bomb, I lifted and looked at each and every box, turning them over in my hand, unsure of what I was supposed to be looking for. It all occurred in absolute silence.

"Which one do you like?" said Mr Parry breaking the tense stillness.

I looked up at Mum with that silent look children can sometimes give their parents of how much can we afford? I think Mr Parry knew and before anything was said he added:

"Well whichever one you like you can have it for £10"

Even to this day my choice, a simple George III horn rectangular snuff box set with a small pewter plaque in the lid, does not distinguish me as a young prodigy of antiques (I was never that), indeed it was probably the most boring of all the boxes there that day, though it was the one I liked the best.

Mr Parry, or Pat as I later knew him, never made his fortune selling me that horn snuff box but he did set me on a path which has lead right up to where I am today.

Every couple of weeks for many years it became the routine that I would leave my Mum and Nan to do the Saturday shopping and walk up the hill to see Mr Parry, always first pressing my face against the shop window to see what was new. Perhaps a mustard spoon or a vesta case or a pill box? I would sit and talk to him and he would tell me the tales of his early years in the Antiques Trade and then give me sound pieces of advice which I would almost always fail to follow.

Pocket money then was (a very generous) £3 a week but most of the things I longed to buy were between £15 and £30 in the shop (even with a generous discount). The solution was simple, I had also been allowed 80p a day at school for lunch (this paid for gloriously cheap deep fried double sausage, chips and a glass of full fat milk). My allowance was more, a whole pound, on sports days (20p extra for a can of pop). The maths was simple, I could wait up to ten weeks to buy something or abstain from lunch during the week and wait three, so three it was. Six and a half years of school lunchtime hunger proved to be the first sacrifice the World of Antiques would ask of me, but certainly not the last.

Pat had seen the golden age of antiques, where every dealer had their "patch", auctioneers were only ever wholesalers and the vast proportion of stock was bought directly from people coming into the shop or calling him out to clear a property. He'd been instrumental in setting up one of the first "proper" regional annual Antiques Fairs (Kenilworth) and had, as a young man, played snooker once a week with a friend in the trade whom he advised on any area he didn't know much about. He even lent him some pieces of early Chelsea porcelain when he was asked to take along items to his first ever TV appearance at BBC's Pebble Mill. You may have heard of him, his name was Arthur Negus.

Pat, whose early career had been in factory production, (his family's firm), once sat me down to look at a Georgian silver caster in the shop. By then I'd had an interest for some years and knew to look at the hallmarks and for damage or repairs but on that day Pat told me to handle the caster and look at the gauge of the metal, feel the sides and thickness, the base and cover. "Look at how these are made, Michael. Look at the gauge of the silver, how they match, the cover and the base."

More by accident than design I've been (almost) everywhere in the World of Antiques since then. Studying it at College, reading every book I could, working at auction houses good and bad, on specialist courses, dealing, but no one has ever told me to look at an item's construction, it's actual physical making in the way that Pat did one Saturday afternoon in his little out of the way shop next to the Odeon cinema. This and his other great piece of advice I'd pass on was simply to "assume everything, everything you see is WRONG until you've proven it's RIGHT".

That advice came after Pat and his wife had returned from a holiday in Hong Kong and vowed (in the mid 80's) never to buy a piece of Chinese porcelain ever again, so convincing were the fakes they had then seen being made. How wise that piece of advice has proved to be in recent years.

The first display case I had, for a small Sunday antiques fair held in the local library, came from Pat, a glazed stained oak case lined with plush red velvet which I used (on and off) for the next twenty years up and down the country. My first copy, tattered, borrowed copy of Tardy came from Pat. In pre Amazon times Tardy was an impossibly difficult to find small guide to World Hallmarks, which is still a good all round first port of call for any foreign mark. But most of all I had taken away the advice of how to look at an antique, any antique, as a puzzle, as a sceptic or a sleuth who had to determine "the right" of a thing not just from how it appeared but from how it was actually made.

Pat Parry may not be around anymore, but his wise words are, more than forty years later, always ringing in my ears.

Chapter 3: My own, my precious...

I had been lucky or unlucky enough depending upon your perspective, to pass the entrance examinations for one of the local Grammar Schools. It was a Victorian red brick monolith, well "duolith" or whatever two monoliths are, conjoined by a series of arches and a long gallery which had been overtaken for storage by the Art Master, Mr Hughes, and his huge Victorian printing press. How on earth he ever got the heavy cast iron limbs of the 1848 contraption up there is still a mystery for the ages, though it probably had something to do with all the burliest fourth and fifth formers pulling on ropes whilst being whipped.

The right hand block was simply floors of class rooms, the left hand block was the same on the ground floor but housed on the upper, covering at least two thirds of the floor space, a large oak panelled library which for older readers I might say was something out of Tom Brown's School Days and for everybody else Harry Potter.

There was a large dark wooden vaulted ceiling with exposed decorative beams and bosses, with high bookcases covering every wall, with two rows of large mahogany desks running parallel to a central clear aisle. Above the bookcases hung large black wooden boards beautifully lettered in pure gold leaf with the names and dates of "old boys" who had variously entered different Universities, interspersed with stern portraits of past Headmasters, Temperley, Floyd, Manton, all the names of the "Houses" new boys were put into, even down to the correct flash of colour in the school tie (I was in Temperley and we sported a fetching dash of purple).

At the top of the library the rows of desks abruptly ended and the bookcases, previously open, were glazed and locked to keep rarer and newer volumes safe, this was now the reference section and the Librarian's huge oak desk with the banks of drawers for the card location system guarded it. It was safe to say that after the tuck shop the Library was my favourite place in the entire school.

Years, both happy and unhappy, mostly unhappy, passed at my school as my real interest in antiques began to blossom. Apart from a couple of books from the Library or bought at Christmas from the local branch of W.H.Smith my only access to any form of education on the subject was watching the Antiques Roadshow every Sunday afternoon.

My Dad had let's say "acquired" a VHS recorder from the pub one dark winter's evening, without box or instructions and it had been left to me to decipher it's workings. It was better than any toy and hard to explain the sheer wonder of recording actual television to anyone who did not grow up in the early 80's.

Once it was operable every single episode of the Antiques Roadshow was recorded and kept, to be watched again and again and again. Not just for entertainment but for education, the only link I had to the world of antiques growing up on a council estate in Birmingham. I'm older and more befuddled now but there was a time when I could have told you, almost word for word, the description, order and value of every single object ever filmed on the Antiques Roadshow, I knew them, almost literally, by heart, because it was in part an exercise of pure devotion.

In the meantime there had been school and school work and school politics. One of the chief pastimes was "getting in" of a morning. The school, a red brick fortress, was inaccessible to its pupils before ten to nine every morning. We would all have to gather in a iron railed and gated "play" ground, stomping and shivering through the winter months, often for an hour if we had to arrive early and often, getting a lift, I did.

The doors were guarded by impossibly smug sixth form prefects who basked in the warmth being churned out by the enormous Odenesque cast iron radiators which must have weighed half a ton each and were permanently hot to the touch. We would crowd up the well worn narrow flight of stone steps to the large gothic arched black hobnailed double doors just in case one of them stuck their head out. Firstly to get a draft of the almost tropically warm air inside and secondly, possibly to "cadge" a way in. Our excuses were many and various.

"I have to hand a paper in, Mr Ratcliffe said I could pop up and leave it on his desk" (unbelievable) or "Quick Pearce has got the runs, he's not well we have to get him to the loo" (urgent, but still unbelievable).

Occasionally it might work which is why we tried, but almost every morning we stood, frozen outside, billowing plumes of iced breath into the courtyard like so many small shivering steam trains. It was a most unsatisfactory state of affairs.

It was around that time that the Geography Master who also oversaw the running of the Library was asking us fifth formers to volunteer to help reorganise and modernise the Library. It was just like when the Officer in any War asked for volunteers and everyone took one step back, what would be the point of undertaking all this additional work?

"You'll have to do it as you can in your spare lessons, lunchtime and whenever you are free." he said to us all.

Whenever we are free? WHENEVER? I thought.
A group of my friends then stepped forward, we were, by the virtue of a single pace, Library Assistants but more than that we were the holders of the keys. Prefects in their casual suits would hold no more threat or bar to us, egress in and out of the large, quiet, unsupervised and eternally WARM Library was ours whenever we wanted it.

It had to be said going meticulously through the entire card index system, re- typing it, adding new books, deaccessioning the older out of date volumes was a mind numbing task, but made all the more bearable that we would be taking at least the entire three terms (before we ourselves were sixth form prefects) to do the task and there was an added bonus. The library floor, one hundred and fifty year old polished parquetry oak, was rich and lustrous and extremely smooth. If you gave the soles of your brogues a very good clean and had a short run up you could slide down the entire length of the unsupervised Library, so that was exactly what we all did.

Two things happened in the second term of particular note. Firstly the older books we were deaccessioning, which I confess I had started to find fascinating, were mounting up in the side room to the library and secondly, well we'll get to that later.

The first problem was to dispose of the books, charity had been mentioned or a table at the school fete, however I thought I had a better idea. We should hold an auction. I'd lot the books up (tied with string) and allow a weeks viewing and then a sale, conducted by myself, one lunchtime. Either everyone thought it was a good idea or simply could not be bothered to do anything themselves, whatever the reason I was about to hold my very first auction.

I was left to my own devices and began sorting through the books. The star lot might have been an entire set of De La Rue encyclopedias which it took three of us to carry in one go, there were older volumes too, gifted by old boys of the school, one of which had been a Principal Keeper of Printed Books at the British Museum. Two volumes, though now distressed, in full rich calf leather binding with gilt tooled decoration, one a History of Herodotus and the other a copy of Homer's Odyssey, had particularly taken my eye.

The second occurrence of note was that on that Sunday's Antiques Roadshow a book had been brought in, it was a copy of J.R.R.Tolkein's The Hobbit, a first edition printed in 1937. It had been inscribed by Tolkein too and had been valued at an absolute fortune (£5000+), I couldn't help thinking it looked familiar.

The next day, a Monday, I got to school early and went straight up to the Library. I scanned the locked bookcases behind the librarian's desk and saw, on the third shelf down, the now very familiar blue, green and black dust cover of The Hobbit. I was however still very sceptical, I was sure our school would not have a first edition. It occurred to me that whilst I could not yet unlock the cabinet to inspect the book and look for the tell tale date, the small corrections in the dust jacket etc, etc, all meticulously and carefully described on the Roadshow the previous evening I could check the card entry for it in the system, they all had the year of publication noted. As I leafed through the index in the small side room, fluttering through musty grey hand typed cards in row after row of light oak drawers I happened upon the entry, sure enough it was dated 1937.

The key to the cabinets was kept by the Geography Master and I should have to see him to get it, I waited until lunchtime to go to the Teacher's Room. "Oh Mr Smith, he's off on a trip for three weeks"

THREE WEEKS! He had not left the key and no one knew where it was. A single pane of glass stood, I thought, between me and the most lucrative of deaccessioned lots in my forthcoming Library Book auction. I sat and looked at it through the glass most mornings, hoping and dreaming that the three weeks would pass swiftly, though indeed they dragged like the passage of an anchored sailing ship loaded with lead.

In the meantime I had discovered that Tolkein had briefly attended our school, not for long, but perhaps long enough to have sent a copy of his new book to the Library? Maybe he had written a short dedication himself, my head whirled with all the possibilities and I was now convinced a fortune, an actual fortune was only about three millimetres away from the tips of my greedy little schoolboy fingers. I had even checked the last person who took it out and that had been over ten years ago, it had lain untouched, unwanted and unknown.

The third following Monday I could not get to school fast enough, there was not a child in England that desired to go to school more than I did, had I got the plague I would have shaken it off and fashioned a crutch and dragged myself in, the Geography Master was in his room early.

"Hello Sir, good trip? Wondering if you had the key to the Library cabinets?"

"Oh, yes, here it is"

He took it out of his waistcoat pocket and pressed it into my grasping little claw.

"Better get going it's Assembly in five minutes"

It did not matter to me if it was Assembly in five hours, minutes or seconds I was only ever going one place, to the cathedral quiet of the Library.

I could just hear the whole school faintly singing Hymns at Assembly as I stood before the glass bookcase, my hand almost trembling as I took the small, longed for, brass key out of my pocket and turned it in the lock. The click of the mechanism echoed around the room only punctuated by a boy's gasp of breath.

The copy was delicately, gently, one might say reverentially taken from the shelf, no damage to the delicate dust jacket, no fading, no creasing, though the accession number had been written on the spine. I opened the pages and there it was, in black and white, my own, my precious and then.

"Reprinted 1978"

There was a loud and audible cry.

It should have been no surprise and it was entirely just. As the assembled tones of the school belted out Hosanna! I saw that my plotting had come to nothing. The last boy to have "taken it out" some ten years earlier, the year the reprint was made, had not brought it back. Rather an impostor, correct in every detail save for the date, stood proudly in its place, I solemnly returned it to the shelves and locked it safe away, ready to taunt another library assistant with just enough wit to be taken in.

The Library Auction was still a great success, some of the lots made a pound, the set of De La Rue encyclopedias sparked a bidding war and ended up at a hefty twenty eight pounds (I suspect parent's money had been involved) and I, I did buy one lot, for fifty pence, which comprised two beautiful if distressed full calf gilt bindings. Though my heart sank a little knowing it should have had one book more besides with trees and snow capped mountains on the cover first printed in 1937 and worth a small fortune.

Was there a lesson in all this for a young boy? It might be if you are given good books look after them properly, it might be that the true value of a book is in reading not selling it (true), but as I am now a low and terrible antiques dealer at least in part, the lesson that I'd pass on to you from it is never be fool enough to think that there isn't always somebody else who's got there first.

Chapter 4: Kestrel House

Today you can switch on your television most afternoons and see a variety of auctions (and I must bear some small responsibility for this myself).

Auctions have become commonplace and familiar, everyone knows what and where they are. Even my beloved cosmopolitan sister, who would rather walk barefoot over broken glass than enter an antiques shop, has bid at auction for those essential domestic fettled odds and ends, country pine monoliths to contain pots and pans, dogs and chickens and (when patience is sorely tested) even the occasional offspring. It was not always so.

My own interest in antiques came out of nowhere and as such I was beginning the race from a standing start. My father was a boxer turned market labourer and my mother cleaned part time and looked after the home, further back than that there were postal workers, miners, bar tenders and agricultural workers branching out from my family tree, but no one, not a soul, with the slightest knowledge or interest in antiques.

The local newspaper was for many years the only source of any information. The classified ads each evening would have notices for local antiques fairs and very occasionally auctions. Let me say now that sadly Sotheby's or Christie's (not even Bonhams) took out a column inch in the Birmingham Evening Mail to announce their sales but fortunately other, more local auctioneers, did.

There was Biddle and Webb in the heart of Birmingham with a carpeted hole on the first floor which someone had once fallen through, saved only from death by the carpet gathering then blocking the hole as they fell, leaving them dangling on the floor below like an overly descended testicle. Then there was Clare's, together with a smattering of auctions held in town or village halls but annoyingly they all held their sales during the week when I was imprisoned at school and too timid and chubby to even contemplate digging a tunnel, let alone working out how to dispose of all the soil.

There was however one exception, one auction which was held every month on a Friday evening, starting at 7.00pm sharp and it was only a mile walk (or a 5 minute drive) from my Nan's terraced house. It was inevitable that this would be my first auction, it was proximity rather than destiny, that drew me to Kestrel House. Though this was not an auction that would be familiar to anyone today.

Kestrel House was on a main road running into Five Ways Erdington. This was Birmingham suburban sprawl at its "sprawliest". Much of it was not that pretty, though once, a hundred years ago, it had been a sought after and leafy Victorian suburb, a village on the outskirts which was just starting to be drawn into the spreading metropolis. There were many rows of 1930's terraces and a few Victorian Villa's set back from the pavement by large walled front gardens. This is probably why Kestrel House itself, when you saw it, came as a bit of a shock.

A late Georgian farmhouse with a large arched brick wagon entrance and barns beside a cobbled stone courtyard occupied an entire suburban corner. It had resisted development since being built, though "improvements" had been made. The side of the main house, which faced out on to the road, had a large rectangular single storey glazed addition, upvc frames with the feel of a naff half sized car showroom when new, but now rundown, patched walls and windows, sticky tape repairs and mismatched squares of carpet, dark carpet which did not too easily show the stains. This it would transpire was the main saleroom.

I would always go to my Nan's house after school to be fed and watered, waiting for Mum to pick me up from work which would be around five or six. So that particular Friday evening it was no problem, for Mum and I, to linger a little longer and go straight from Nan's house up to the auction.

It was winter (from memory their sales did not take place in summer, were they on their holidays perhaps?). Already dark and bitterly cold, we jumped into the car and drove the few minutes up to the already busy side street along from Kestrel House to park. It was novel to be out in the evenings, under the orange glare of suburban streetlights hand in hand with Mum against the bitter cold, wrapped head to toe in scarf, hat and padded coat walking up to the first auction I'd ever attend, full of trepidation and brimming with excitement.

We were not alone as a crowd of twenty or so people hurried through the stable yard archway turning left into the farmhouse through a huge thick panelled black painted door, which would have graced any Gothic tale. The first unexpected thing to hit you as you stepped in from the freezing cobbles was the heat.

Directly to the left of the door was a large Georgian fireplace and it was piled, almost to the top, with a mountain of red glowing coals immersed in flame, radiating a tremendous heat that hit you like a wave as you entered. This was clearly partly in regard to the thin pale elderly man who sat, speechless and stone faced, behind a plain wood table directly facing the door and so close to the fire that had he had any blood in his veins it would have boiled, but he was pale enough for that not to be the case.

He had one long skeletal hand placed upon a stack of A4 pages periodically stapled at the corner (catalogues) and in the other a steel cashbox in which he placed the 50p elicited from everyone who passed the threshold irregardless of age or stature. When he took your seven sided coin there was more than the air of Charon the Ferryman about him, he did not look up.

We walked quickly past the raging fire before the wool in our clothes could catch alight and immediately found ourselves in the rectangular "saleroom" which was bordered by ten or twelve trestle tables groaning under the weight of several hundred oddments. Alongside the tables, perforated picture boards ran across one wall sporting some of the worst art ever to be conceived and painted by any living human hand. I knew very little about antiques at the time, but there is a level of dreadful which demands, or more properly requires, no explanation.

I looked around as Mum stood watchfully behind me, I picked up not very old Staffordshire figures, a Tang Dynasty horse from a local takeaway, odd pieces of glass and china, bayonets, brass candlesticks and a very few little pieces of twisted and bent Edwardian silver. It was busy with dealers, who at that time all smoked like chimneys, as the air in the room began to thicken into exhaled swirling blue grey clouds.

I saw from looking in the catalogue there was furniture too and that had to be somewhere else. We pushed back through to the front door (it was now very busy) and back into the relief of the cool cobbled courtyard which had accrued dealers standing in small huddles chatting away. Just beyond the house was a large broken down old Barn and beyond that a small open field or orchard.

Furniture was stacked throughout the Barn in rows. Pine trunks (stripped of course, this was the 80's), dark 1930's oak gate leg tables with barley twist stretchers, odd chairs, overmantles, bedside cupboards and all manner of household items. A few minutes was enough and we returned to the now jam packed farm house as the auction began.

Two men, the auctioneer and a porter walked into the middle of the room as the porter placed an upturned wooden box onto the floor upon which the auctioneer ascended. Clipboard and pen in hand, proceedings quickly began. There would be no buyers premium (in those happy early days I did not even know what that was) and when you bought a lot the auctioneer would write your name down if he knew you, if not, you would bellow it out amidst the smoke filled chatty throng as best you could.

Bids flew in at two, four and six pounds for items which I would not have the courage to be openly seen placing into a skip during daylight today.

My own Mother, now swept up with the excitement (and very much to my surprise), bid a weighty "four pounds" for an oil painting lotted with three others. The "tortured horses" as I christened it on the drive home, was a frightful rendering of three contorted white horses in a circle on a vibrant green ground. It rested for a month or two atop a wardrobe before being quietly discarded, though it was so horrible I now wonder if it was some forgotten Brutalist masterpiece, or an early Bacon worth fifty million or more. It is hard to tell with modern paintings as the line between brilliance and horror is very fine indeed, in fact that line can be as thin and fine as a signature and nothing more. It will serve me right if Mother knew best after all.

As the auction continued I waited patiently for a Staffordshire figure of W.G.Grace to appear, although a shocking fake it appealed to a young schoolboy and I bid a hefty twelve pounds to secure it, though the embarrassment came as I struggled to make my name heard to the auctioneer.

I called out a faint "Baggott" but he looked at me puzzled and replied:

"Abbot, as in Church young man?"

I instantly shouted my reply as loud as I could back:

"No, Baggott as in Pub!" (I shared my surname with a well known hostelry just down the road)

The auction broke out in laughter as the auctioneer looked a little peeved. We left after a couple of hours with our treasures (the tortured horses and Gracie as he would be forever known) and I'd been bloodied. It wasn't quite like the Spartans throwing their youngest into the wolf pit to see who'd come out alive, but it was close.

Mum and I returned to Kestrel House on many subsequent Friday evenings over the years though I never really bought anything of value with the exception of some Georgian silver spoons, years later, which can only have ended up there by sheer chance. I realise now, looking back, it was an ingenious way of selling, piece by piece, the contents of boxes of oddments bought at other auctions during the week for very little indeed. Even if every one of the three or four hundred lots every evening sale only averaged out a tenner it was not a bad wage for doing very little and it was probably a fair bit more than that.

Sadly if you go to Erdington today to look up this Brigadoon of auctions you'll find no trace. The joke of course was that the farmhouse, the cobbled courtyard, the rickety barn, the muddy orchard and the hideous extension occupied quite a plot of residential land. At some point it was worked out quite how big that plot would be and how many tiny little flats and houses could be built on it and the money, the great deal of money, which that would bring. Kestrel House stands no more and the conditions for it to exist and function have gone. Now it is an internet age with a million antiques quite literally lying only a fingertip's reach away.

Sometimes I think I was unlucky not to be one of those children who had dealer parents who took them straight away to the best fairs and auctions, I think how much quicker and further I may have gone. But then I think how much, that first night back from Kestrel House, we all laughed because of Mother's awful painting of the horses, and laughed again and again for years to come. It's not for everyone but there's a joy in making all the mistakes from the very bottom up, which I now wouldn't trade for anything else. There was a pleasant peasant joy in going to my very first auction not at Sotheby's or Christie's but at Kestrel House.

Chapter 5: Big trouble in Big Brum

"There's an antiques fair down the market tomorrow" said Dad just home after a full night shift, "We can go if you like"?

My interest in antiques had only been going for a year or so, with only regular weekend visits to the local antiques shop and the odd Sunday table top fair, everything was still quite new and largely unknown.

My family treated the whole thing kindly, but with an air of gentle suspicion, except, that was for my father, who quite honestly had no interest in it whatsoever. It was like trying to explain rocket science to a duck, entirely pointless and a waste of both our time, so when he offered advice on an antiques fair, out of the blue, everyone was shocked and disbelieving.

Muttering "he's got the wrong end of the stick" Mum checked the local paper and yes, oddly there was an antiques fair in the middle of Birmingham's Rag Market on a Wednesday morning. This all seemed quite wrong, but it was half term and the offer had been made by my Dad, so why not go and find out?

The fair was advertised as starting at 7.30am so Dad and I got the earliest Bus we could to the town centre, the 6.48 and with all the stops, it would take a good half hour to get us there.

As we arrived in the city centre Dad tightly gripped my hand as we got off the Bus, he knew Mum would have killed him if he'd lost me. The Terminus was only a short walk from the Birmingham Wholesale Market, and Dad proceed to dash off at quite a pace, pulling me tightly behind, dodging through the already bustling crowds of market workers, crisscrossing each other's paths at speed whilst pulling carts laden with boxes and pallets of fruit and veg up and down the streets, weaving between one another in a clattering fury of activity. The pavement was strewn with cabbage leaves and potatoes that hadn't quite made it, crushed once or twice under a heavy market labourers boot they proved quite a slippery hazard, as well as filling the air with a strong vegetal scent.

My expectations of the "Big Brum" had not been great, in fact I was still not entirely sure there would even be a "proper" antiques fair (as I then knew them) in so rough and odd a place. I was completely unprepared for the sight that greeted me as we came close by to the huge metal warehouse in the Market Centre.

Dealers, HUNDREDS of antiques dealers, were crowded around the four (North, South, East and West) entrances to the building. Some were there waiting to get in and buy, with frozen hands thrust into great coats and leather jackets or clasped around polystyrene cups of tea, all jostling against one another, moving in waves like shoals of wary mackerel trying to avoid the net.

The majority waiting to enter had a stand to set up on one of the hundreds of trestle tables arranged in rows inside. They pushed along carts or wheeled boards with boxes of stock, precariously stacked as high as they dared, all tied on with rope. The noise was a deafening clattering of a thousand trolley wheels going over broken kerbs and uneven tarmac, all above a throng of banter, laughter and swearing. Prices were being thrown out as people grabbed and pointed at items they could spy on the carts as they passed by, rolls of money swiftly fluttered in and out of pockets, brown tens, purple twenties and rare red fifties, thick rubber-banded rolls of notes, each of which could have easily choked the largest of Donkeys. "Watch out for pick pockets" my Dad sagely advised, as I plunged my hand into my coat and grabbed about thirty pounds of saved pocket money very tightly indeed.

It was exciting and I have to say a bit overwhelming.

"Go on" said Dad as he pushed me forward and I entered the scrum as the noisy steel shutters were raised and everyone launched themselves into the large trestle tabled space, like the start of the Grand National.

Bedlam was quieter than this. Some dealers, familiar with the chaos ran directly to see others "who had something put aside for them", whilst others just entered the fray, as boxes of stock were simply up ended onto the rows and rows of trestle tables in heaps. Dozens of hands thrust in, picking up objects left, right and centre, with screams of "how much?" Replies came back with equal speed "fifty", "eighty", "two fifty", "a grand"! Antiques were then tucked into pockets and cash exchanged, if you thought the trading floor of the stock market was as frenetic as business ever got, think again.

That first time I went, as a boy with my Dad, I didn't quite last five minutes. I was too small and was elbowed, kicked and pushed out of there, at least three dealers trod on my foot in the space of a minute and I'm pretty sure only one of those was accidental. That, together with the fact that I didn't have the slightest idea of what I was doing, was enough to scare me off the Big Brum for a year, but that was only the beginning.

Time passed and I'd gone to slightly bigger fairs and got slightly bigger myself, big enough and strong enough to push back and much more importantly than that, I now knew what to expect and I would be "braced for impact".

I'd realised that the Big Brum was one of the largest fairs in the Country. It was on my doorstep and unlike many other great fairs (Newark, Ardingly) it was completely free to enter. Dealers from London came up in specially hired coaches and did deals long before the fair started in the cafes nearby, mostly under the table, mostly dodgy. The outside stalls set up from 6.30am and that was the first battle of the day.

As each dealer stood behind their stall putting items out one at a time, a crowd, two or three people deep, running along the whole available front of each stall, leant in and pushed, constantly pushed, reaching forward to grab each item as it came out. It might be too much for the first hand, or the second but it rarely got past the third. Think of seagulls dive bombing unsuspecting tourists for their chips, it was that level of persistence, every tasty morsel was quickly gobbled up.

I took to the fray. You either swam or sank, never mind the manners you'd been taught all your life, get in, push and elbow your way in, but get in! People would scowl and frown as you eased them aside, they might even manage an indignant "excuse me!" but you didn't fall for that, you just kept pushing.

Silver dealers in particular had the habit of carrying their stock loose in large tubs or containers. They'd tip them out into a large heap in the middle of the bare wooden table and you'd just thrust your hand in like a lucky dip. As soon as you got something you liked the look of, you'd raise it up in the air, catch their eye and often before you could say "how much?" the price would come back at you. How they knew the price astounds me to this day but that's how it worked.

During my "school years" I could only go when the fair fell on a holiday as it was always midweek, on a Wednesday. I never found real treasure in those days but would always buy a handful of things, oddments across any discipline of antiques you could care to mention, a Chinese tea bowl, a pair of Georgian turned mahogany spill vases, a plain Nathaniel Mills snuff box, an Irish Glass butter dish, all for a few pounds, all with a profit in them (when years later I started doing small antiques fairs myself). You never, ever lost money on anything you bought there, that perhaps was why everybody pushed quite so hard.

After college I returned home to try dealing for a while. I could now drive, had a car and spent every day touring around and about at fairs, shops and auctions. Clearly the "Big Brum" would be on the list and for the first time I went to the fair with confidence and money, I should have known it wouldn't go to plan.

It's been rebuilt now but the original Rag market building had a side road running around it. If you got to the fair early enough (in darkness) you could just about find a place to park a car and leap out, torch in hand, to scour the dealers carts as they gathered around the outside of the building, waiting for the doors to open.

It was six o'clock, winter and pitch black but I'd driven in, determined to make an early and fruitful start. Annoyingly all the regular little places I knew to park had already been taken, so I did another circuit (the road around the building was in a large loop) and found a patch of wasteland behind a nearby building to park without a yellow line in sight. I jumped out and, with a few hundred pounds in my pocket (which honestly felt like a million) began to scour the market, inside and out.

The sun rose as the striped shopping bag I had with me (all the best dealers had enormous hard wearing shopping bags mostly used by Pensioners, I'd borrowed this one from my Nan) got fuller and fuller as Dawn broke. There was an early Georgian Sheffield Plate salver (£35), Georgian helmet shaped cream jugs, a Scottish silver caster hallmarked in Edinburgh 1760 (£95) and countless small caddy spoons and knick-knacks, a proper haul. By then my legs were aching and I wanted to get back to the car and drive home for a full English breakfast and a proper survey of the spoils.

When I got back to the car in daylight, only then did I see the small but clear "Private Parking" sign next to the bit of wasteland I'd left the car. It was now boxed in completely by five or six other vehicles and the only sign of where the drivers might be was a grubby grey door at the back of an industrial block which backed onto this unofficial "Car Park". Without any other option I approached and knocked upon the door, at which point, flimsy as it was, it fell open.

The space behind appeared to be a busy kitchen of sorts, steaming large pots were bubbling away and rows of burners lined the space as the centre of the room had upturned boxes with ten or twenty Chinese gentlemen, waving and shouting, playing a game I wasn't familiar with alongside frankly huge sums of money. They immediately fell dead silent at my untimely arrival and were quite evidently less than pleased to see me.

I was, (I assume) then sworn at loudly in Cantonese by no less than ten different people at once, as the one nearest to me grabbed a meat cleaver of startling proportions and proceeded to waive it expertly in my direction as others followed behind him brandishing a selection of equally imposing kitchen utensils, Ready, Steady, Cook this was not.

I tried, by the international language of pointing and shouting (and possibly weeping) to explain that the little red metro was mine and that I'd very much like to go now, in fact as quickly as possible, but it soon became apparent that was not an option. Once I'd backed away sufficiently, the door was slammed shut with a loud cry from inside which I took not to be a blessing. I was in the "Car Park" bag in hand and walked to the nearby Terminus knowing I had to take the Bus home and the bag was getting heavier with every step.

Some hours later, and with the Dad in tow for "muscle", looking as menacing and tough as he could look, we went back. The high stakes game, whatever it was, was over and my car was eventually retrieved with a measure of embarrassment and profuse misunderstood apology.

As we drove away I took some comfort in knowing that this would surely be the worst, the very worst thing, that could possibly happen due to a visit my still beloved "Big Brum" and that I would make sure it, or anything like it never happened again. Of course I was completely wrong. This wasn't to prove the worst misadventure at the fair by some considerable margin, but that day, driving home in my "Chinese Takeaway" of a little red metro I was happily oblivious of worse things yet to come.

Chapter 6: Fear and loathing in Over Whitacre

"There's an auction on today up the road" I said to my Mum across the breakfast table.

Suffice to say this was so long ago that I can't remember if I hadn't yet passed my driving test (third time-slow learner), had passed but couldn't afford a car, had passed but had sold my car to buy an Irish sugar bowl and cream jug (true story) or couldn't afford to be insured for the one we had. What was certain was that my Mum would, within reason, drive me anywhere an antiques fair or auction was being held.

It was a Sunday so other things, important things (the roast dinner) needed seeing to first.

As Dad was still working at the Birmingham Meat Market, a rib of beef the size of a small toddler, was entombed in tin foil and squeezed into the oven with matriarchal heft and determination, being left to cook on the lowest of heats for several hours until just the touch of a fork would cause the tender shards of meat to tumble off the bone. All the vegetables were peeled and ready to set to boil upon our return and a large bowl of batter for a dozen Yorkshire puddings stood resting, ready to drop into blistering hot beef dripping at the very last moment. Having done all the work that needed to be done we could now set off to a village hall somewhere (somewhere?) near the hamlet of Over Whitacre.

We got into the car and I grabbed the local "A to Z" off the back seat, it would almost tell us where to go. We drove off the main road which turned into side roads, then into lanes, then into country lanes then just muddy tracks. Even on the map a stray hair could have been mistaken for the narrow roads we were taking, though ultimately, after a few wrong turns and about half an hour we reached a small roadside sign which announced "AUCTION HERE TODAY" with an arrow pointing into a muddy part graveled drive. It was surrounded by broad leafed trees dappled yellow-green through the beams of morning sunlight playing upon and through them.

In front of us was a small village hall or pavilion, distinctly Edwardian in tone with an open veranda and small porch bordered by ripening fields of wheat on two sides and the road on the other.

Catalogues, single stapled A4 mimeographed sheets, were 50p each at the door and Mum reached into her purse before I could check for change and bought me one, Mums always do that, well mine did.

Upon entering the Pavilion you could see a large central hall with a side room to the right divided by a sliding partition which was half pulled back. There were a few people congregating around a small canteen doubling up as bidder registration and the accounts office (a cash tin and a ledger). Happily it served cups of tea and biscuits with a small seating area to the side with plywood stacking chairs and melamine topped tables to sit at. It could have been a school fete, a cricket luncheon or bingo, but instead it was a Sunday village auction. The sort that sadly do not seem to exist anymore.

The main hall had rows of tables stacked with bric-a-brac, old sporting goods, wooden ski's, golf clubs, bowls, etc. There were boxes of Victorian ceramics and glass, odd brassware and copper with darkened oak furniture, washstands, hall stands and chairs running around the walls, though I really just wanted to look at the "smalls". These were all in the side room, housed in two long locked glass display cases and comprised any jewellery, vertu and hopefully some silver.

The porter manning the two cabinets was a short older man with a balding head and two stiff shocks of hair at the side, glasses perched on a sharp beak of a nose hiding small beady black eyes, I thought I recognised him though he did not say hello.

I should say now that whilst I would have gone to view this auction for a Sunday trip out, I did have a particular motive for going. The sale was advertised as comprising "residual items" from the estate of a peer of the realm (who's son was a well known actor). The question you're now asking is if that's the case how on earth did it end up in a Village Hall in the middle of nowhere?

It's often the case that the "BIG" auction houses will offer to clear an entire estate for a family to get their business. This entails going into one or more properties and taking down all the fine paintings, the good furniture, the silver and jewels though it also means clearing out the kitchen cupboards, the fridge, the toilets and the outhouses and you'll never see the Head of a Sotheby's department pulling on a pair of rubber gloves and getting stuck in.

In these cases a firm of clearance auctioneers or dealers get subcontracted and it falls to them to physically and entirely clear a property of whatever detritus it may contain. The exciting part is that often families over generations put things in odd places. Jewels in bags of frozen peas (for security), odd broken chairs from important sets in the potting shed and any manner of family gew-gaws in forgotten bedroom cupboards which are then wallpapered over. This then is what I hoped (but not expected) to stumble across on a Sunday afternoon in a village hall in the middle of nowhere.

The smalls were very disappointing to begin with. Six Victorian teaspoons one lot, a beaten silver vesta case another, then three small paste and gilt metal watch fobs, all very ordinary, it looked like this way just going to be "a day out". Then the porter passed me the next small plastic bag, this was much more intriguing, two "YELLOW METAL" watch fobs, but these were clearly unmarked gold and each set with a beautifully engraved armorial carnelian seal, certainly for the family of that particular peer. I paused to circle the lot in my catalogue and looked up to see the porter briefly disgruntled. I continued to look at every lot and found a pretty Chinese silver box (circled that too) then got to the last bag.

Mum came over and said "Have you seen what you wanted?" Just as I took the final lot out and started to look at it. I turned it quickly over in my hand, once, thrust it back into the bag without any fuss and turned to her. She saw I had gone slightly ashen faced and knew the look. Saying nothing I simply motioned to the door with my eyes as I started for the car park.

"How much money have you got?" I asked her when we were out of ear shot.

"Only the shopping money for next week, and a bit put by for Christmas" she replied a little warily.

"Well I've got about a hundred and then another two in the Bank."

Antiques obsessed as I always was in these situations the arithmetic had simply taken over and already I was trying to work out how much I could possibly beg, steal or borrow, even if we had to starve next week and cancel Christmas.

"Would Nan lend me some do you think?" I asked as we began the drive home.

"You'll have to ask her." Mum replied sternly. Indeed I would.

"So, so what is it?" Mum asked with the air of a loving but exasperated mother who had been here before. She knew the signs very well, besides I've never had a poker face.

As we drove home I began to feverishly explain, in the very excited way that anyone who loves antiques does, that I had walked into a Village Hall and been lucky enough to pull out of a horrid plastic bag a piece of silver which had to be at least two hundred years old, if not three.

It was a combined child's whistle and rattle cast as a lion wearing a crown with traces of mercurial gilding, all suspended on a superb cast open work chain with scrolls and a single pendant bell. There were no estimates in the A4 stapled catalogue but it had to be worth at least a thousand, possibly two and I was now desperate to buy it.

The auction started at 1.00 pm and by that time I had begged and borrowed, from every relative I could, to get me up to a bit over six hundred pounds. The buyers premium back then was either 10% (yes I know just 10% kids, the glory days) or £1 on any lot selling under £20, that meant a bid of £550 was pushing it but possible. I now had several hours of nervous waiting, fearing that the £550 bid just wouldn't be enough. Believe me, nothing is as bitter in the world of auctions as not having enough money to go on bidding when you know it's the right thing to do.

Sunday dinner had to be postponed (that almost never happened, Dad was beside himself) and we drove back to the Village Hall as it got busy with local dealers and people out for a weekend afternoon jaunt. I sat at the back of the cafe area with Mum nervously looking on, sipping tea and sharing a Kit-Kat, waiting for the lot to come up (it was about 300 lots in). As the auction began it seemed like it was going to take forever.

As a distraction, first up would be the two gold armorial fob seals catalogued as yellow metal. I was a bit worried about bidding for them at all (it would lessen my bid on the silver lion) but you have to try for everything. First the paste seals came up and I was surprised to see the beady eyed, sour faced porter bidding on those and getting them for £30, they really were rubbish, though oddly he seemed very pleased to have bought them and was grinning ear to ear. Next up were the lot of two unmarked gold fobs which I'd hoped had been missed. A flurry of bids took them up to £50 but then it stopped to my surprise, I put my hand up at £55, then £65, then after an odd bid from someone else £80 had done it and I'd bought them. I was delighted and it helped calm me down, first blood at any auction will do that.

I went back to Mum at the cafe table, smiling and said they had to be worth £300 at least (a fortune at the time), though tension still began to build back into my bones as I thought of the lion whistle to come and how much less I would now be able to bid on it.

The auction proceeded and prices varied, some things seemed to make much more than they should which did little to settle my nerves. As we got to only a few lots away Mum turned to me:

"You're not going to get carried away bidding are you? You mustn't be disappointed if you don't get it."

Though she said this knowing full well that I always got carried away bidding and was then always bitterly disappointed if I didn't get it. I got up from the table trying as nonchalantly as I could to lean against the wall, unnoticed (failing miserably), in eye-line of the auctioneer so my bids would not have to be too obvious but also not be missed. There was a pause as the lot I'd waited a lifetime for (or so it seemed) came up for sale. There had been a couple of phone bids on lots throughout the sale which surprised me and I hoped, prayed, the auctioneers weren't waiting for one on the silver lion.

The auctioneer announced from his small wooden podium:

"Next lot a lion, white metal, not tested, what am I bid?"

I paused with my breath held tight.

"Twenty, Ten then, alright who'll start me at a Fiver?"

My hand raised very slightly, just enough for the auctioneer to see.

"Five, Six, Eight, Ten, Twelve now. Are we all done at Twelve pounds? Twelve pounds then to the Gentleman standing, going, going, gone!"

I numbly raised the card paddle I'd got before the sale started as the auctioneer noted down my number and I turned to face my smiling Mother at the table as I silently mouthed "TWELVE POUNDS!" in disbelief and stumbled forward, stunned at what had just happened. For a minute or two all I could think was "twelve pounds!" though in truth it would be thirteen when the one pound minimum buyer's premium was added.

We didn't rush off as I remembered the Chinese box and bought that for a similarly wonderful and ridiculous six pounds (plus again the one pound premium). Then I hurried off to pay and claim my prize. After paying I got my receipt and handed it to the porter. He first handed me the seals I'd been so pleased to have bought at the start of the sale.

"I'm sorry these aren't the right ones, I bought the two yellow metal seals" I said.

The now even more beady eyed porter, who I'd now managed to place, he was a local dealer I'd seen at auctions, clearly moonlighting today, replied:

"No, I bought those, these are yours"

I pointed to the catalogue I'd clearly marked and then saw that the adhesive labels on both bags had been peeled off and put back on. The loathsome little goblin had switched them, no wonder he'd been smiling when I thought he'd paid too much for the paste ones at £30.

I complained to the auctioneer straight away but the porter aggressively and loudly stuck his oar in and the auctioneer, who was no match for his employees fervent protestations, simply shrugged and said he was sorry for the confusion. He agreed that if I didn't want the lot I could get a refund straight away, though that really wasn't any consolation at missing out on those two gold seals.

Sadly there's not a lot you can do when this happens out in the wilds. It could have turned to name calling (starting with "bastard" and going on from there) or even fisticuffs but there's never really any point to that, besides I had those other two lots I really wanted to clear.

A refund was given straight away and within minutes of the debacle I returned from accounts (the cafe) to pick up my two lots. The odious porter was there, I'm sad to say, smirking away at the stroke he'd just pulled. He grudgingly passed me my little Chinese box, then paused as he held up the lion whistle in its plastic bag, like a schoolyard bully who'd just stolen your lunch,

"Suppose you think this is old then, do you?"

he half mocked as I rested it out of his hand.
I took it and went to leave but paused and turned back, drawing close,

"No" I replied "I bloody KNOW it is"

though I may have said another word for "bloody" and with that smiled and left, never looking back, though I would have dearly loved to wallop him.

As Mum and I drove away from the village hall, bound for a late but delicious Sunday roast dinner I put the gold seals behind me (they were after all not the "main event") and instead sat beaming in the passenger seat holding up my beautiful silver lion whistle on its heavy chain in wonder and disbelief as we hurtled along green and sunlit country lanes, heading home. That was, I think, more than thirty years ago now.

I'd like to tell you that the porter got his comeuppance. I'd like to tell you he slipped coming out of the village hall and was crushed by a rogue tractor then his twisted remains eaten by foxes, but he wasn't, they never are. The antiques trade is littered with a small handful of desperately unpleasant people whose sole purpose is making money by any means necessary, be it swapping lot numbers on bags or things far worse to mention here. You can only ever do your best to recognise and then avoid them and be happy in what you do. Certainly driving around the country with my late Mother at the wheel, near or far, I couldn't have been in better company or happier.

Since those early days I've learnt that these combined silver whistle/rattles in the form of a lion are a type that appear rarely on the market, sometimes they are catalogued as Spanish, sometimes Dutch (and I suspect the scope of the Hapsburg Empire has more than a little to do with that). What's indisputable is their age, of this particular form (though there are later versions) which are seventeenth century in date. I can also say, with a degree of certainty, that in the ensuing years since no one has ever bought one at auction for less than £13.

Chapter 7: The Antiques Job

Sometimes, no matter how hard you personally go out of your way to derail things, fate takes a hand if it thinks the fit is right. I don't come to this conclusion out of pure speculation, I come to it out of experience.

Many years ago, at College, studying Fine Art Valuation, the first year was coming to an end and those who were not going on a trip around the world, or surfing in Cornwall, had found employ at the great and grand auction houses and galleries throughout the land. It was only a coincidence that their fathers, mothers or uncles worked for those same auction houses and galleries, pure coincidence, as most of them couldn't even say nepotism let alone spell it.

Even my closest friends had managed through charm and grace (two things I so severely lacked that I doubt even Canova could have carved them for me), to obtain summer positions with "notable" people in the trade. World class restorers and wealthy dealers.

It was all quite depressing and it looked like I was going home for the summer to watch what little there was on TV.

We had just one more college trip to London to look forward to before we broke up for summer. Ostensibly we would, as an entire year, travel up to London in a coach to visit a museum, any museum (The Soane, The V&A, Chiswick House etc, etc) though we would in truth simply scatter, doing whatever we wanted for the several hours before the coach left on the return leg.

Some might visit "friends" in town, others would set off on an expedition worthy of Sir Edmund Hilary to find the most delicious Baklawa they could. Others would simply drink themselves into a stupor, whilst a few of us would rampage through whichever auction might have the misfortune to be on view at the time. On this occasion the dubious honour fell to Christie's South Kensington and their unsuspecting silver sale.

Rowdy students going in mob handed to a quiet viewing unnerves some people and five or six mouthy students is near enough a riot in the quiet red carpeted environment where only Angels fear to tread. (an "Angel" being the name for a kindly retiree who was placed on the view to pass items out of cabinets and keep a beady eye on troublemakers).

I discreetly misappropriated an unguarded and untethered saleroom copy of the catalogue (sorry Christie's but you should have chained it up) and proceeded to view knowing full well I was just about skint.

So it was bitterly disappointing to discover a fine Irish silver two handled cup marked for Joseph Johns of Limerick, so so very rare, estimated for pences. Even though the estimate of four to six hundred pounds was criminally cheap, try as I might I simply couldn't think of any legal way I could afford it, I'd already burned through my student grant at pubs and bookshops. This was also assuming that it might sell for within its low estimate and in the middle of London, in a saleroom surrounded by generations of razor sharp silver dealers, that probably wasn't going to happen.

The Coach ride back was a slightly solemn if lightly drunken affair (we found a pub after the viewing) full of disappointment over being too "out of pocket" to bid for the Limerick cup despite having spotted it. Not even one of the world class Baklawa being generously handed around could cheer me up.

The next morning, over cold Pizza for breakfast, ordered from a cheap local takeaway which we ALWAYS called Leonard's to the proprietors annoyance (Leonardo's) an idea, a crazy idea, one of the few good ones I've ever had struck me and this is where I think fate lent a hand.

I cheekily wrote to then then Head of Silver at South Ken with a short CV and a request if there were any work experience positions still available for over the Summer. To put this in context EVERYONE I knew had written to Christie's and Sotheby's to begin with. The two great auction institutions were really and truly harder to get into the Fort Knox and everyone who'd asked had received a polite but terse "NO" whatever their family connections might have been. But I had a secret weapon up my sleeve and it wasn't my pale white arm but my bare faced cheek.

At the end of the standard student request I added the observation that one lot in their forthcoming sale, a Limerick silver cup, was woefully underestimated at £4-600. I went on to say that it should make at least two thousand pounds, and if it did the very least he could do was give me an interview. Cheeky little...fellow that I was, well what had I got to lose?

You could back then (before anyone knew what the internet was) call a number printed on the inside of the catalogue to receive the sale results for CSK. It was either a highly sophisticated automated system which cost them millions to install, or one of the Directors maiden Aunt's, with little better to do than sit by the phone knitting, who had been paid a tenner to read them all out. I happily waited ten minutes for them to get to the result of the only lot I was interested in:

"Lot 202 (the Limerick cup) sold for £2,200"

The miracle that I had hoped for, born in a room full of Angels, had happened. I received the letter a few days later asking me to come up for an interview over lunch with the Head of the Department.

The interview went well, as all we talked about was antiques and antiques had always been my favourite and only topic of conversation. Unimaginably I had leapt out of the jaws of no work experience whatsoever to a prestigious Summer Internship at Christie's, all through the dumb luck of seeing an Irish silver cup and just about knowing what it was. Here fate gave me a helpful nudge, though in later years it was really going to have to push.

My first paid full time position, my first actual job in antiques was far more haphazardly acquired. After leaving college I had applied for a job as a general valuer at Sotheby's and had got down to the final two, but sadly the victor had been a previous Sotheby's employee and an untested youth wasn't going to beat that. A couple of months passed and then another position became available, that of running the silver department, this I hoped would be my chance.

Inbetween college and looking for a "proper" job I had been dealing in the smallest way imaginable, out of an antiques centre in a Wiltshire town, a converted church which had been divided into more than a hundred glass cabinets, one of which was then mine.

I'd first taken it with two student friends and we'd shared the rent and the space placing in little odds and ends we'd pick up from carboots and weekend town hall fairs. It went quite well, probably because of the mix of porcelain, silver and treen, every odd little bit. It had gotten to the stage when Terry, who ran the centre, said our little cabinet was often the first port of call for many of the regular dealers who passed by, though that possibly had more to do with underpricing everything, than the cabinets curatorial merits.

The day of the interview for the job as "Head of Silver" (all the other body parts already been conveniently taken) fell mid week and over a two hundred mile drive away from home. I hadn't been to the cabinet for three weeks and it seemed sensible to combine the trip to restock, even though it was a little out of the way. I left early and was at the centre for nine in the morning when it opened.

Opening the boot of my little Mini Metro (£500 and capable of speeds up to 100 miles per hour on the open road) I took out a box of odds and ends I'd gathered since I'd last been down. Odd bits of Georgian brass, a bit of early Continental porcelain (a Vienna eculle richly painted with fruit but lacking it's cover if I recall rightly, bought the Sunday before as a Victorian fruit bowl for six or seven pounds, now priced at forty) and sundry silver items of course.

I walked up the Yew lined path to the old church door as Terry saw me approach, box in hand, he pulled open the heavy oak door of the centre for me. I rested the box on the counter and said a good morning.

"Good week for you last week, glad you've come to restock" said Terry.

"Great, how much did I sell?" I eagerly replied.

He thrust a wad of around seven hundred pounds into my grasping little paw, more, considerably more, than I had ever taken.

I restocked and after a short conversation and a quick look around the centre and nearby shops I set off for my interview at Sotheby's.

At this point I should mention that the "pay" at a major International saleroom was not there for you to live on. It is (or certainly was) assumed that you had private or other means to sustain your lifestyle and pay for luxuries like food and rent. The salary offered was simply a token kindness for everything you'd be doing, not a living wage. I was considering all of this and the seven hundred pounds I had just picked up, a bundle of thick old purple twenty pound notes sporting an image of Shakespeare, stretching the slender fabric of my smart trouser pocket. I stopped on a country lane, in the middle of nowhere, in front of a beautiful old Georgian brick building with a bright red telephone box nearby and made the call.

"Hello, yes I'm just calling to say I shalln't be attending the interview after all."

My free hand curled around the money in my pocket as I spoke.

"I've had a change of heart, hope you don't mind, thanks so much...bye"

I put the receiver down after talking to the third of fourth most senior member of Sotheby's staff and drove happily home. Being free, with cash at half past eleven in the morning, stopping at every antiques shop I passed by for a quick ferret around seemed like bliss, it seemed like living the dream. Regret only began to percolate in when I arrived home and everyone, everyone was utterly aghast at what I'd done. Still fate's plan was not so easily derailed.

Two days later, after I suspect all the other candidates for the position as "Head of Silver" had been interviewed and wholly failed to impress the phone rang.

"Good Morning, Michael, yes I was just wondering if you'd had a change of heart and reconsider popping down for that interview tomorrow?"

This time I went as you don't get a third chance and even getting this second one was pretty spectacular. Mum came with me, ostensibly she said to help with the driving, but in reality to smack me round the back of the head with a thick rolling pin should I suffer a similar change of heart and try to about face in the car.

The interview went like a dream and I got the job, as Head and every other bodily part of silver, which I held for just about four years. Stepping into it as Mr Blair won his first election and everyone was singing things could only get better and for a time it genuinely seemed like that might be true, particularly as the Fish and Chip shop only a five minute drive from the saleroom was truly world class.

Perhaps Fate has a way of sorting things out, though I probably don't believe it, but in one way perseverance might. Before college, before Christie's, before

Sotheby's in the long gone dark days just after leaving school I had, I must confess, been unemployed. I had been unemployed for quite some time, nearly a year of my earliest youth wasted. I tried to get a job in an auction house, any auction house or dealers shop that would have me but failed and was forced to the fortnightly ritual of signing on, which robs you of your pride and of little bits of your soul.

The six monthly review came as I sat before the lifeless, joyless, heartless job centre manager for work advice, being told I should give up any desire to be in antiques, that is was both stupid and wilful to insist upon it, that it was clearly never going to happen.

The suggestion was that I should consider a position in an office, any office if one became available. I shudder to think how many other dreams died on those job centre notice boards.

Perhaps if you don't give up, perhaps if you are obstinate and hear your calling and believe, in yourself as much as anything else, perhaps eventually fate will take notice and lend a hand, no matter what ends it has to go to.

Chapter 8: Your leg bone's connected to your mouth

A series of unlikely events had lead, inexplicably, to me "running" the silver department at Sotheby's, albeit the little regional one down in Sussex that often got left off the list of "International Departments and Offices" in any of their really important sale catalogues.

Sensibly though I was not left immediately to my own devices, a member of the glamorous, "Starsky and Hutch" style side of the business, the valuations department, had worked in the silver department in London for years and was to supervise me and instruct me in the arcane ways of the World's oldest Auction house (please nobody say "Christie's").

"Blum, Blum, Blum, Bli, Blo, Blo…"

I heard over my shoulder as I realised I had made the cardinal error of typing "Candelabra" instead of "Candelabrum" which is the correct singular as anyone who knows their Latin declensions will tell you.

"Sorry Matthew, yes I know" I replied.

"Just keep an eye on it and get those boxes sorted and catalogued by the sale deadline next week"

When I said I ran the silver department, perhaps I should have said I just did most of the donkey work.

"I'm going up to town next week, you must come with me and I'll introduce to everyone in the department and we can take that seal case up too and get their opinion on it"

The few weeks I'd been there I'd been a quite happy little fish in a little pond, tip tapping away at my computer cataloguing weighing and measuring all manner of silver shiny things. Now I was to spend the day in London with the great and the good of the antique silver world, the real giants, and my mind (and stomach) turned at the fact that I was never really good at meeting new people.

All the great London specialist departments are a little less glamorous than you might imagine and certainly a lot, lot smaller. My then own office of a shared room in Grade I listed country house which I believed "adequate", proved by comparison, palatial.

Imagine any standard office you've ever seen with slightly older wooden desks but every surface, the shelves, drawers, bookcases, floors covered and I do mean covered with fine antique silver.

I was quickly introduced around and then led to the office to the side where the Head of the Department worked.

"So what have you got there?"

I had brought along an unmarked seal case, a silver tube, like a cigar case but with two ends for keeping sealing wax and possibly wafers (not ice cream), one of the covers had been finely engraved with the owner's Coat of Arms to impress into the molten wax upon sealing a letter.

"Right, let's look the arms up, you've used Papworths before?"

I hadn't, I didn't even know what Papworths was (it is a guide to British Heraldry) but shame and cowardice sealed my lips firmer than any wax from the sealing case we were researching ever could, so I simply nodded.

For ten excruciating minutes I was left to fumble alone through the pages of Papworth in the corner of the office, desperately looking, hoping the identity of the Coat of Arms may just fall open at a random page, of course it didn't.

"Well they don't have the tinctures (colours, denoted by different engraved or stippled grounds on silver) on a lot of the seventeenth century Armorials so they can be tricky" said the Department Head.

I don't know wether he believed that or not (though I can say now it is actually true) I suspect I'd been given a graceful way out.

"Yes, it's difficult to pin it down" the relief was palpable in my voice.

"Well enough of that I must take you chaps to lunch".

Naively I thought we might be popping downstairs for a sandwich, I'd no appreciation of how serious a thing "lunch" was, far more serious than identifying the Armorial on a seventeenth century seal case. As we readied to leave the building someone lifted up a silver mounted Chinese famille verté porcelain pot at the end of the room and called out to the Department Head.

"Before you go?"

"Where's it going?" he asked

"Geneva"

"12-18,000 in Swiss francs and remember its Paris discharge (mark) for 1684-7" he replied.

We then all set off and I was thinking HOW VERY COOL it was to be able to quote estimates, off the cuff, in various international currencies.

We darted swiftly through a couple of nearby streets, until coming to very smart Georgian town house, descending towards the basement to find a gentleman's club (no strippers) with the ghost of P.G.Wodehouse still running through it.

It was dark, really dark and smelt mustily of what I imagined the Victorian Era might have smelt of, it was an historic odour. The porter who took our coats was at least that old, thin and immaculately dressed in a military style uniform that wouldn't have even fitted him when he was a young man. I gave him my coat, the weight of it lurched him forward (it was not a heavy coat) to the point I feared he might topple, but years of doing just this had hardened him like tensioned steel and he immediately sprang back into position.

"Let's get a table" said my colleague.

We were escorted to a booth in the middle of the "Club/Restaurant" and the department Head divulged "The Lamb's very good here". I was in no position to argue, so we all ordered "The Lamb"

I sat beside my colleague from valuations and opposite the Department Head. They were friends of old and I'd decided the best course of action was to shut up, pay attention, smile, nod and eat my free lunch as they caught up with one another.

The meal came, it was a quite large passable lamb leg chop with potatoes and veg, a nice posh school dinner. A leg chop was indeed a treat, we had never had those at home only the fatty thin chops which you crisped up, (which I loved) and gnawed at, long after the plate had been cleaned, there would be none of that home style gluttony today.

I can't honestly say I remember anything that was said, all I know is I paid keen attention at the time, maintaining a look of real interest. My focus sadly had been diverted from where it really should have been, my focus should have been on the lamb leg chop on the plate in front of me.

If you blindfolded someone, giving them a knife and fork and asked them to do it I don't think the odds are 1 in a 100, maybe even 1 in a 1000. Without looking, my fork had entered the very middle of the chop, the soft dead centre of that hard white leg bone without any resistance and the knife, the knife had cut it free without scrapping or touching to elicit a warning, I stuffed it directly into my mouth.

Here I was with one of the most important figures in my industry, treated to lunch, treated as a colleague, as an equal and I'd just unknowingly stuffed a whole fucking leg bone into my mouth. I began, as best I could to imitate a chewing motion whilst breathing heavily through my nose as my other airway was now completely blocked.

Neither dining companion looked away. All I needed was a moment, a single moment of privacy to hurl the thing out but it was not coming. Seconds felt like hours but I was still determined that swallowing a lamb bone whole would not be my personal and professional epitaph. I readied the napkin in my left hand having placed my knife down and waited. The Department Head went to elaborately blow his nose and my colleague suddenly looked away.

I spat out the bone (now white clean through nervous mastication) with such accuracy and speed into the waiting napkin by my side that I'm surprised there wasn't a round of applause, though thankfully nobody had seen.

The rest of the day is hard to recall, though we never did find out to whom the Armorial on the silver seal box belonged and neither did I journey back to town with my colleague ever again in the following few years I remained at Sotheby's. I didn't ever want them to be put in the position where they might give me the chop, well, not another Lamb one anyway.

Chapter 9: Cup of tea?

Recently I had a sobering thought about how a "big birthday" was now not so far away, looming like a stray horseman of the apocalypse galloping directly towards me. At least he was still in the saddle, confounding current medical thinking, or at least the specialist who told me, years ago, with a look of puzzlement that "I really should be dead".

This maudlin looking back was further encouraged as a colleague in the trade dropped an off hand remark that he had watched me talking about antiques on TV as he was growing up, GROWING UP?! Was I that old? Yes, I double checked I WAS almost that old, albeit that he was very, very young. It put me in mind to think, really think about the one piece of advice I would want to pass on to an up and coming youngster in the world of antiques and auctions, that golden phrase which you could cling to, the mast to which you would tie yourself in a Siren storm.

A flurry of obvious, almost trite sayings played across my mind. "Study hard", "Always buy a good book when you see it and then remember to read it", "Say you don't know when you don't know", the list ran on, but mulling it over I thought these were all quite obvious, what was the real insight that I could give from my own unique experience? The one thing I wish, looking back, that someone had said to me starting out as a fledgling auctioneer all those years ago? Then it all came flooding back, the visceral horror, I knew at once what the advice would be, words to live by, words that might save your life as an auctioneer:

Always politely decline a cup of tea if it is offered.

I had joined Sotheby's after leaving college. A job opened up only when all the other specialists played musical chairs. That is to say the head of silver at Bonhams went to Christie's, the head of silver at Sotheby's (Billingshurst) went to Bonhams and I plugged the gap.

There really isn't that much to do within a specialist department. The running of the auction house, the real headaches, are dealt with those higher up, which is why they were always paid so much more. A humble specialist only had a handful of duties. Catalogue the lots, prepare the sales, auction the items and, when asked to, go out on valuations.

Cataloguing was my main occupation and it was all quite high tech for the 90's using Sotheby's in-house computer software called "S.T.A.R.S" which stood

for "Sotheby's something, something, something..."
well you get the gist.

I would call up a clients details, add the lots to the
system and catalogue them, adding all the sale details
by ticking or filling in various boxes. There was one
box which occasionally, when you entered the clients
account number, came up with the letters "VIP". It
could mean a variety of things, from a titled family, to
a Hollywood film star but mostly, mostly it meant that
a person had sold a very valuable item at Sotheby's
and that the red carpet should be rolled out.

My own feelings on the "VIP" box were indifferent in
as much as whoever you were, a Saville Row suited
Duke or a pig farmer covered in muck stained
overalls, if you came to see me within working hours
for advice or an opinion you got the same courteous
service. I was quite communist in that respect, "all
clients were created equal" besides it was often the
pig farmer that had the better item to sell.

I had not been working for more than a few months
when a call came through from a gentleman living on
the South Coast. He had some items he'd like an
opinion on and could I come out to see him, he said
he'd sold with us before. Upon checking his account
details that magic "VIP" box came up and although it
was going to be a bit of a drive, I knew I'd have to

make the trip and duly arranged an appointment later in the week.

I'll confess now that almost all my valuations, where possible, were tabled for a Friday and a Friday morning at that. If they proved worthwhile I had time to come back to the saleroom with the spoils, if not I could immediately head back home for a long weekend and get an extra half day off. That may sound appalling but in truth my weekly work could all have been done in a day, that it lasted a week was more a case of spreading it out so you didn't get bored.

Departing early I set off with the address and a bundle of local A to Z's to guide the way (Sat-Nav was still a dream). After a few country lanes and pretty costal roads I pulled up to a bungalow overlooking the sea. The position was wonderful the building not so much, but "VIP" guided me to think this would all be worthwhile.

As I knocked on the door I heard a gruff male voice faintly swearing to "shut those fucking kids up, someone's at the door!" and for a moment I thought I'd got the wrong address, but I hadn't.

"Hello, Mr Baggott? Yes come in"

The middle aged man greeted me and I was shown through to the sitting room, whilst tripping upon and then roughly kicking aside any number of small plastic toys strewn liberally across the floor.

On an Ikea table stood some odd inexpensive pieces of electroplate. I inspected them with due care and attention, whilst secretly delighted that I may very soon be setting off for an early weekend. I began to describe the date, the maker (where possible) and to run through values punctuated only by the screams of the children I could not see, but whose toys I had thoroughly booted into touch on my way in. As I explained that the items "would not be for us" in as a gentler way as possible, it was here I made my fatal mistake, it was here that an unremarkable home visit became unforgettable. The man leaned forward and offered me a cup of tea. I foolishly, carelessly, recklessly replied "Yes".

A couple of minutes later I was asking what else he had sold with us, more than ever mystified by his "VIP" status but determined to get to the bottom of it before I left. It was then his wife arrived with a mug, my mug, of tea.

The mug was white but not entirely clean, thin stains of a previous beverage, at least I hoped that's what it was, streaked down the sides in rivulets of foreboding. This should have prepared me for sight of the tea itself, though it really, really didn't.

The surface of the tea was a meniscus of misery, a swirling rainbow of colours like oil on water interrupted only by a floating armada of irregular platelets, like small icebergs crashing together, driven by an unseen tectonic force. I desperately hoped it was no more than limescale from the insides of a neglected kettle, I hoped that.

Their eyes were fixed on me and smiling as the mug was placed before me. They were not bad people, they were just bad, very bad, at making tea. Sadly I was there with my official Sotheby's hat on, so I knew I was going to have to drink it, if not all of it, at least a few polite sips.

I touched the handle of the mug and it felt slightly greasy as I lifted it up to see the lively flora on the surface of my beverage dance and flutter in the raking light, hoping I had just glanced a reflection and not a stray eyelash.

The edge of the mug touched my lower lip and I tried as best I could to "strain" the surface impurities through my moustache and teeth so they would not poison my body. It was indeed in the strict material sense, a cup of tea, though it did not taste of it. I managed two further sips over the next five minutes whilst nursing the mug in my hand, making an apparent show of my interest in it, whilst keeping it firmly at an arms length.

The couple had, I found out, sold a book which had belonged to his father, an early Incunabula (a printed book prior to 1500) which had made over thirty thousand pounds some years prior and that had been the origin of his "VIP" status.

As I got up to leave I thanked them for their time, apologised that their items weren't valuable enough for us to enter for sale and remarked on a "lovely" cup of tea, though perhaps I should have said "unforgettable", possibly "unforgivable". They were both happy and I knew at that moment that if they both genuinely believed that I had enjoyed my tea there was no lie I could not convincingly tell if I ever wanted or had to.

Young auctioneers I tell you now ALWAYS politely decline a cup of tea if offered and if you don't, be it on your own head.

Chapter 10: A length of green wire

In the time between Christmas and New Years it had become the custom for Mum to drive me to the local antiques fairs. My childhood fervour for antiques wasn't shared by anyone else in the family, if anything there was a degree of disapproval and suspicion which greeted every purchase. It was only twenty or so years later that my Mother began to accept I might (I stress "might") just know what I was doing, though from time to time I still made a purchase which would frame that view as charitable optimism.

I had gone to College, gone to London, gone to Christie's and then finally gone to Sotheby's. After a few years of serving that sentence I was freed and went back to where I had always really wanted to be, back home to start over as a humble "totter" of gewgaws and trinkets, as one dear friend in the Trade was apt to say "shiny tonk".

I'd departed near the end of the year so was looking forward to Christmas at home before striking out anew and fell quickly back into childhood traditions, one of which was going to the local post Christmas fair.

Mum was always happy to come along. She'd grown to enjoy these adventures, these odd days out, driving to far flung parts of the country she'd never have visited otherwise, although now she could be the relaxed passenger as it was clearly my turn to do the driving.

It was two days after Boxing Day and we'd all been cooped up eating chocolates and watching TV for far too long. The big local fair at the time was held at the Stafford Agricultural Showground and even though it was a good forty minute drive it was a welcome escape.

We left at just turned seven as the fair opened to the trade at eight thirty and I always wanted to be near the head of the queue. The car was covered in thick ice and the only option had been the plastic top from a can of Mr Sheen, deployed to scrape the windscreen clean. As I glovelessly scrapped away, plumes of powdery ice covered my bare hands turning them numb and red with cold. I climbed into the car and jammed my frozen paws straight over the now hot air vents to get some sensation back into them before we set off. I could just about begin to feel the steering wheel.

We drove, mostly through quiet country roads then lanes, passing the three spired glory of Lichfield's cathedral, then the voluminous industrial wide mouthed power station cooling towers of Rugeley which stretched up to swallow the sky. All the time the steep hedgerows leant in, painted white with cold and plastered with frosty diamonds glinting in the low winter Sun.

The Showground appeared on our left. The main building for the fair was set back behind a livestock paddock with a short uneven road which was blocked off to public cars. We parked on the nearest patch of field and got out to find it slippery underfoot.

I edged around the car to grip the paddock rail. The grass was fine but the road up to the hall was thick with black ice and back then I always wore my tweed jacket, waistcoat and highly polished smooth soled brogues which were poorly suited to the conditions. Mum's footwear was more sensible, winter boots so she was fine and walked a little ahead, I slipped over a couple of times but landed with little damage showing there was at least one advantage to having a fat arse.

The queue was already about twenty dealers long when we joined it and there was still another ten minutes to wait until it opened. We stomped our feet a little and made our plan of attack.

The fair was separated into three halls. The first was a proper glazed and carpeted venue. Here the "better" dealers had their wares. There was always one long stand of good quality Victorian furniture (fashionable at the time) with stands of porcelain, silver and general antiques. I knew there were two silver stands in particular that I would go to first and I told Mum where to meet up, as whilst she would walk in, I would run. The next two halls were really just corrugated steel agricultural sheds, used for livestock during the normal course of business. The second hall had more dealers selling oddments and Knick-knacks though the quality was still ok, the third hall, unlike Goldilocks porridge, was not "just right" but usually filled with tat, repro, second hand books and house clearance furniture.

I was particularly excited by this fair as unusually I actually had some money to spend. Sotheby's had paid me my monthly wage "retrospectively" which I hadn't realised at the time. Although I'd left the month earlier I still had one more pay check to come. It was a lovely surprise and whilst not a fortune it lay resting in my account waiting for the opportunity to be wasted on something, anything, shiny.

As the fair opened I dashed in and quickly did a

circuit of the first hall, darting straight to the first two silver stands and then circling once more in case one of the general antiques dealers had something interesting, all I could find were a pair of lovely but horrendously overpriced cased Georgian paste shoe buckles which no amount of haggling could make buyable.

Disappointed I began to walk around the other two sheds with Mum. I knew that the real chances of buying something decent were always in that first hall, now it was all about a day out and maybe finding an odd spoon or pair of Georgian sugar tongs for a tenner. We ambled around the rows of table top stands, nothing leapt out and I was ready to go but Mum, wise as ever said "we're here now why don't you do the last hall?" She was right of course, why not?

The last hall was rarely fully booked and so dealers spread items around to make it look a bit fuller. Half size plastic figures of Betty Boo and ghastly reproduction lamps which would have made Louis Comfort Tiffany spin in his grave were mixed in with resin Art Deco bronzes and horrific modern "collectables". We'd almost finished quickly walking around the last hall when we were greeted by the sight of one stand which arrested my attention.

The stand was one of the standard wooden topped folding tables which the dealer had not even bothered to cover with a cloth. On it stood three rows of plates, all graduating in size from small, medium to large. Each was of recent manufacture and had been transfer printed with various "adorable" pictures of kittens. The smallest front row of kittens were priced at £2, medium £3 and the largest a heady £4 but this was not the curious feature which had taken my eye.

The back left leg of the stand, a tubular metal leg had been wrapped many, many times with a cord, in fact a length of green plastic coated garden wire. The wire looped in and around the leg and then shot up in a wild arc before half disappearing behind one of the largest kitten plates where it seemed to attach to something small, something glinting. I walked around the side of the stand to get a better look at what was hiding there unaware the stall holder was now alert to my presence and on his guard.

"What do you want mate?" He grunted which took me slightly by surprise.

"The wire, the wire" I pointed to behind the plate,

"Can I have a look?"

Perhaps because I had on my tweed jacket, waistcoat and shiny black brogues the ruffian acquiesced and passed me this carefully wire entombed treasure.

The wire was twisted around the end of the stem a spoon, a silver spoon. To anyone who does not know about spoons this had a deep curved fig shaped bowl and a straight faceted stem with a seal top finial, this was, though I couldn't quite believe it at first, a very old spoon.

Before I had chance to ask, the stall holder recounted the tale.

"My mate went to an 'ouse sale a couple of weeks ago"

(I should point out here that the "House Sale" was not the contents of some Stately noble pile in the country as you might see at one of the leading London salerooms, but the sale of the contents of a house, i.e a fridge, a cooker, a settee, a TV etc)

He continued: "He bought a tray of kitchen cutlery and that was in it. Four quid he paid for the lot but he asked me to bring this along today for him. He took it to Sotheby's and they said it might be high hundreds."

I didn't like the last part, the fact it had been "taken to Sotheby's" but what he really meant was that he'd shown it to a Sotheby's regional rep which actually wasn't that bad.

Reps (there were a dozen or so) all had their bit of the country and they held valuation days and worked their social connections to get stuff into the departments for sale. Whilst working for Sotheby's for the the few years I did, I found reps knowledge of silver to be a "gently working" one at best and most of the time the pieces they got in for sale came in with either alarmingly high or attractively low sale estimates, the one for the spoon I felt might be the latter.

"Can I just check something?" I asked the stall holder, as I nipped back to one of the book stalls further down that row. I hadn't thought to bring my own hallmarking guide and needed to be sure that what I was looking at, was what I thought I was looking at, namely an odd standard mark, a familiar lion passant but one which was wearing an odd little crown.

After checking and pausing for a moment to gather myself I returned to the stall and asked the simple question, how much?

"£900" came the reply and despite a bit of pleading "£900" was it.

"Take a cheque?" I brandished my cheque book and a bank guarantee card and the reply came back

"No, but I'll take three"

Duly and to my Mother's absolute horror, as she looked on, I very quickly wrote out three separate cheques for "£300" (clearly the stall holder was hamstringing his colleague, but hey-ho) and spent my last months Sotheby's pay on a quite badly dented but heavy old silver spoon.

We returned to the car with my Mum asking me "what I'd done that for?" and "why I'd spent all my money?" I simply clung to the paddock rail as there were still thick patches of ice underfoot and I didn't want to land and break the spoon now laying in the inside pocket of my tweed jacket, right next to my heart.

I cleaned the spoon carefully when we got home and then fetched out my large copy of Jackson's and began to explain my moment of madness to my Mum.

The first town mark had been applied to silver in around 1300, the first date letter in 1478 and that alongside the maker's mark were the three punches which made up a hallmark. It was not until the reign of Henry VIII, due to various debasements of the coinage, that another mark was adopted, that of a lion passant to show the object made was of sterling standard and for the first few years of its introduction it bore a little crown.

Unbelievably the spoon in the third worst hall, wrapped in a length of green garden wire and hidden behind the kitten plates had been one of the very first pieces of English silver ever to bear the lion passant. It was marked for the very first year it was used, 1544, in the reign of King Henry VIII and despite a dented bowl it was a very lovely spoon and the best thing I have ever bought before or since at any Antiques fair.

Later the following year I did my first "big" Antiques fair and foolishly sold it. I got a good price for it, a price that delighted my Mum who had still been quite sceptical about its purchase despite my explanation. But it was sold before the market for early spoons really took off. Today you would be fortunate indeed to buy it for less than ten or fifteen thousand pounds, today you would be fortunate to find it at all. Regrets? I've had a few, but top of the list was selling the spoon I found wrapped in a length of green wire.

Chapter 11: We have found the drawer

A client (Gerry to his friends) had said he'd be in
London for the weekend, this, the fact I had
something to sell him and an auction to view in South
Kensington conspired to meeting him in my car
parked in the side street by Christie's on a Sunday
morning, just before they opened for viewing, too late
for breakfast and too early for lunch.

The pair of rare Newcastle sugar tongs I had brought
to show him carefully and religiously wrapped in
acres of acid free tissue paper had fallen on stony
ground. I was barely able to get them away for what I
paid for them so it promised to be a thoroughly
disheartening day.

"Well, now shall we go in and view?" said my client
(nowadays a firm friend) as he stuffed the tongs into
the inside pocket of his Barbour coat with so much
eagerness I felt I may have fallen for the oldest ploy in
the book, that of feigned disinterest.

"Yes, there's a collection of spoons I want to go
through"

"Great, you can do that after but first you can come
round and view the furniture with me"

Looking back perhaps I should have turned the key in the ignition and sped off back up the M40, perhaps it would have been better if I had, but instead I walked through the portico of the now much missed CSK (Christie's South Kensington).

Auctions were going through a hard time and Christie's had hit upon the idea of "Interior Sales". So long the bastion of the Specialist Department, drenched in decades of 'glasses perched on the end of the nose peering down at you' expertise that every breath of air had its own catalogue description and lot value, but vulgar market forces decided that had to change.

The top management had slowly begun to realise that the majority of its wealthiest clients lacked any significant degree of intelligence or the merest spark of imagination. Buyers could attend a specialist sale for a piece of furniture that they wanted but then completely fail to recognise that the vase offered in the specialist Ceramics sale the week following would sit beautifully, if purchased and placed upon it. You may think from my tone I'm making this up, but believe me I'm not.

The answer they felt was the "Interior Sale" (Antiques for Dummies).

Here furniture, porcelain, silver, decorative arts, metalwork, carpets, paintings would all be mixed together and displayed in room settings, just in case you didn't know the carpet went UNDER the bureau and the mirror ABOVE that. Frighteningly they were a great success.

This meant that on view on this particular day were not only a desperately badly catalogued collection of early english silver spoons, but a selection of early english oak and walnut furniture.

"I've always wanted a good walnut chest" said Gerry "and they've got about seven or eight in for sale"

I knew a little about furniture. I'd learnt it at college, but that was a few years ago. Being fundamentally lazy I had always thought it better to deal in spoons which fit in your pocket than linen presses which fit in your van and only then after you've struggled to carry them there.

"Look this is a nice one, good colour, what do you think?"

What did I think? I didn't know what to think, was it good, bad or Sergio Leone? But I had to show willing.

"Yes Gerry, it's quite nice, but shouldn't we look at them all?" was a reply that went some way to disguising my ignorance.

I proceeded to nod and agree as he rounded the saleroom, pulling out chest of drawers after chest of drawers, tipping them forward and back to check the feet were original (most weren't) and opening and closing every drawer to see that none of the handles had been later replaced (they all had). We came to the second to last one which was in for a bit less than all the others, by now I had started to form opinions based on no knowledge whatsoever and pre-empted the inevitable examination.

"I like this one." I blurted out.

"This one?" replied a slightly mocking voice.

"Yes, its nice, a nice colour, I know I'm not a furniture man but I really do like it" it was my sincere but uneducated opinion.

Two or three brisk minutes passed as my companion pointed out ALL the things that were wrong with it, handles, drawers, restoration. I nodded and then bid him farewell as I went off to view the spoons I'd come for and never gave the furniture a second thought.

Four days later, just after the auction had been held in London (I'd bought two fabulously rare spoons from the sale, but more of that another time) I got a phone call from Gerry. As I picked up the receiver, I just heard:

"You Bastard"

"What?"

"You utter Bastard"

"What, why, what have I done?"

"That chest, that bloody chest you liked at Christie's do you know what it's made?"

After I'd left the viewing my friend had bid on a couple of the chests he'd seen at the sale, getting neither, they had all fallen within their estimates, £3,000-£4,000, with one exception.

"It made £9,000 you jammy bugger, three times what the rest did!"

I had confirmed by an actual sale result that my gut instinct on a piece of furniture, which I knew absolutely nothing about, had been right. Of course I twisted Gerry's tail, winding him up a little much to my own delight, but unbeknownst to me the damage had been done. The seeds had been sown for me to countenance spending MY OWN MONEY on a piece of antique furniture.

Weeks passed and the furniture infection lay dormant in my system, it was all spoons, spoons, spoons. Until the fateful day I viewed one online catalogue.

It was a country sale, the sort you have to go through with a fine tooth comb just incase "renaissance masterpiece" has been confused with "Zanusi washing machine", there was nothing of interest except, near the end of the sale an early walnut chest of drawers. It reminded me of the Christie's examples weeks earlier with a few notable exceptions, it had no feet and some of the veneers were missing and, most alarmingly the top right drawer (it was two short over three long drawers) was missing.

I thought the colour was nice, really nice and the handles sort of looked ok and the estimate, only £100-200 was certainly tempting, but what was the point of buying an incomplete chest of drawers?

My CSK companion confirmed that replacing feet was commonplace but "getting one made" (the drawer) was a fools errand, it would cost a lot of money and be brand new once it was done, so the piece would never be "right". I knew it was common sense and thought no more about it, though I was still sorely tempted to buy it if it only made £100.

It was the weekend and the morning of the auction for the chest of drawers. Almost half the auctions that happened those days did so with online bidding (now they all do)! You would wake up, log on and sit in the comfort of your own room with tea and toast as the auctioneer proceeded at a snail's pace, mainly due to everyone who was bidding slowly from the comfort of their own home, online, sipping tea and crunching toast.

Warnings would flash on the screen instructing you to "bid quickly" or giving you "fair warning" (that the auctioneer was getting fed up, wanted his lunch and was going to hammer through the next ten lots like lightening). Occasionally you might even get small corrections to the description, "this is not the correct image" or "please note: 2 not 3 in the lot" (one must have been nicked during the viewing). I had seen them all before, but was not prepared for the small one line correction I was looking at for the walnut chest:

"Buyers Please Note: We have found the Drawer"

My jaw dropped. The importance of this was not to be underestimated. Firstly this had to have come from a private not a trade source as no dealer with a pulse would forget to put a drawer in the chest that they were selling, I've still never met one that stupid. Secondly they had only just found it, so every dealer who'd gone and viewed and might have left a bid on it wouldn't know unless they were hovering online, like me. I decided if ever there was a time to buy a walnut chest of drawers this HAD to be it. Any idea that I simply didn't have a clue what I was doing had long since gone and my finger began, repeatedly, hitting the button marked "BID".

Well the seller got a nice surprise. I'd bid £600, six times the estimate for a broken bit of wood with no feet and bits missing (but not a drawer). Add on premiums, shipping and it was not far off £800. It arrived the next day and everyone who saw it, friends and family were open mouthed in disbelief and horror.

Then I was luckier than I ever deserved to be. I'd met a restorer who believed in reviving but not "walloping" furniture, who knew his trade inside and out and "quite liked" the chest.

"What should we do about the handles?" I asked him when he was looking it over.

"Leave them on, after all they are the originals that have been on it for the last 340 years" he replied.

Fairpoint I thought as I stared firmly into the workshop floor peering fully into my own chasm of ignorance, I gathered my thoughts quickly and replied:

"Just do whatever you think needs to be done"

A month or two passed and then I was told the chest was ready. Simple feet had been made out of discarded period timber and the whole just gently cleaned and waxed. When it was delivered back no one's jaw hung open in disbelief and that habit Arthur Negus had of stroking the top of beautiful antique piece of furniture became infectious to everyone who saw it. It glowed as all good antique furniture should.

It had been a bargain and I had been luckier than I ever deserved to be, but that was not the final price to be paid, a furniture bug had bitten me and the cure was only ever going to be more furniture. Now I'm surrounded by four chests of drawers, a chest on chest, a secretaire base, a tripod table, a side table, a lowboy, two chairs, a deacon's chest and a mirror. There is hardly room to breathe, but that only goes to prove that good Antique Furniture can take your breath away.

Chapter 12: The parable of Mrs Harriet Pickney Horry

Today in the antiques world bidding or buying in far off lands is only a click or a swipe on your phone away but it wasn't always so easy.

Go back to the start of the decade and you can tell tales to your children of having to disconnect your phone line and plug in your M-O-D-E-M, the magic box which would connect you to the rest of the world, albeit very, very slowly.

"Buying Online" was the last Wild West Frontier, a few desperate folk travelled down a 56mbps dial up connection into unknown, dangerous and unfamiliar lands. I was in the first digital Wagon train going West, I was in the first Wagon.

Every "proper" antiques dealer said that buying anything without being to handle it was absolute madness. Every antiques dealer who now has a Paypal account, Website, profile on 1st Dibs, Instagram account and Twitter feed. Yes they all said they would NEVER BUY or SELL online. Yet by my reckoning back then there were only three of us, skint, mad and desperate, that really knew about antique silver and took the plunge.

Today we are spoilt for our choice of online platforms, with auctioneers struggling to keep up. You will hear the auctioneer at every sale, "I have 20 on the saleroom, 30 from Live auctioneers, 40 from Bidmaster, 50 from Dave in the corner sipping from a cold cup of Tea". In these early days there was only really one online marketplace, it was American and it was EBay, "blessings be upon the name of the profit".

However it wasn't the glossy global streamlined entity of today's TV adverts with smiling, beautiful young people selling bicycles in bright Ebay logo coloured clothing. It was rougher and tougher, spit and sawdust, full of prophets crying in the wilderness and people just crying at their profits.

It had different parts to it, the best one which is now sadly missing (Requiescat In Pace), the one that was to prove the wildest frontier, was a live platform for auctioneers in the USA to list their sales.

You might be able to bid online through EBay on sales, it was down to the individual auction house policy, but it meant, for the first time these auctions could be accessed without actually being wealthy enough to fly over to the States.

I suspect even then some 10 year old had begun to sow seeds of mistrust in oversea's online bidders by logging into their parent's account and emailing in fictional bids of $85,000 on Picasso vases, much to the distress of the auctioneers when it came time to pay. They were all beginning to get a little wary of bidders they couldn't actually see.

The great advantage for us dealers was that America is such a BIG place and didn't have the same auction house dynamic as the UK, where you are literally only ever six feet away from a specialist auctioneer waiting to pounce on you to consign and catalogue your late Father's collection of Wade Whimsies.

Americans had come over to the UK with fat wallets for decades, bought some of our best and worst antiques, taken them back to obscure ranches and apartments and conveniently now, largely from a fast food diet, they were all dropping down dead.

The local auctioneers handling these estates simply did not have the expertise to know what they were selling when it came to good, genuine antiques. Though they did have the business sense to be the first in the World to put all their sales online, through EBay live.

Years later, when everyone bought online, a friend asked me, "how did you search to find these things?" I revealed the simple secret to him. "I looked at everything." He looked puzzled at my answer, "but there are tens of thousands of listings a week?". I stared back and repeated slowly "I looked at EVERYTHING".

This was a throwback form the early days of Ebay. Getting up at 6.00am, logging on and beginning to scroll through page, after page, after page of listing. Stopping by noting down the time of the listing and then going back and picking up where you left off, nothing was missed. Was I OCD?, Mad? No it was very necessary as no one really knew how to describe what they were selling, the Elizabethan Mortar I'd bought as a "Victorian Shaving Bowl" had taught me that.

It was in doing this relentless sifting of listings that I found in North America a general antiques sale, it had a bit of everything, which meant Coca-Cola advertising, carnival glass, folk art, rusty tools and a small selection of "sterling". It was impressive how such a large sale could be filled almost entirely with objects which were about as antique as the computer I was using to view it, but one lot was the exception:

"40 bottle tags, various $100-200".

If you were to go to a meeting of the Wine Label

Circle at one of the better London addresses, walk in and start calling them "bottle tags" I'd give you about five minutes to live, but this Americanisation of the proper term (Wine label) was common enough on Ebay.

Most of the Wine labels in the lot were run of the mill, very run of the mill, a handful of plain Georgian London examples, more than a few Victorian American ones just stamped "sterling", nothing to set the heart racing, nothing that is apart from the two unmarked, "white metal" labels nestling half covered over in the image, my heart skipped a beat and I back then I was young enough for it not to require medical attention.

What you need to know at this point is there exists something known as the "Master List". This is a printed list compiled by successive members of the Wine Label Circle where EVERY variation of EVERY name ever seen engraved on any Wine Label is listed. For some the completion of the list is a life long obsession. Even then it was almost impossible to find any example not already recorded...almost.

The two fabulous urn shaped labels were clearly late 18th century and American Colonial, the thumbnail picture of them just leapt off the screen and slapped me like a whole ten pound salmon across the face.

Each was beautifully engraved "Golden Cordial". I rushed to dig out the tattered, photocopied A4 stapled Master list, the tip of my finger hurriedly ran down the pages "G, G, G..." no, there was no Golden Cordial recorded, BUT I was only half way there. Could they have been re-engraved (a common practice with old Wine Labels) with the name of some horrid 1920's liquor? It was unlikely but I need to find out what Golden Cordial was and more importantly WHEN it was made.

After a few hours and much throwing and piling of books in my then exclusive executive office (end bedroom) I had my answer and had "met" Mrs Harriott Pinckney Horry.

Writing in Southern America in 1770 she had recorded numerous recipes with several for alcoholic drinks, one which was named "Golden Cordial". An entry in the Oxford Encyclopedia of Food and Drink of America records:

"most robust is Mrs Harriott Pinckney Horry's recipe for Golden Cordial, which infuses lemon rind and flavourings in undiluted Brandy"

The actual recipe which I dug up a little later sounds far more appetising, if prohibitively expensive to make:

"one gallon of brandy infused with citroen or lemon peel, sugar, almonds, peach kernels, cinnamon and cloves are allowed to sit in the sun for several weeks before being strained and bottled for use"

So all the hard work, I foolishly thought, had been done. I'd found the lot, researched the name, established the period and provenance and it wasn't lunch time. I was only a step away from Wine Label Circle fame, all I had to do was buy the bloody thing and a group of frail old men in their 70's would attempt to raise me up on their shoulders whilst singing ballads celebrating my discovery. Images flashed through my mind of being unceremoniously dropped on the floor as their replacement hips gave way, for anyone dedicated to antiques life really couldn't get much better than that. It was then that I tried to leave a bid online but was refused, odd I thought? No problem though, I'd call through when it was morning over there and just leave a MASSIVE bid so I'd know I'd get them.

I called and spoke to a bubbly, bright, desperately unhelpful young lady working at the auctioneers:

"Hello. May I leave a bid with you on lot 233?"

"Have you bid with us before?"

"No, I saw the sale online and am based in the UK"

"I'm afraid we can't accept your bid from the UK, Sir"

"Well, it is for rather more than the estimate if that makes a difference?"

"How much sir?"

"Well the lot is on for $1-200 and I'm happy to leave you $4,000"

"One moment Sir...(long pause)...we would need you to transfer the $4,000 to our account to accept the bid"

"Pardon? What?!"

This was not the age of "one tap banking". Walking into the local Branch of my Bank asking to do "International Transfers" had already elicited some funny looks from the staff. Is he funding an international terrorist cell? Money laundering for an international drugs cartel? Buying dirty books from Amsterdam wholesale? Ignoring the attendant shame and suspicion which came with every international transfer I'd already made, the actual reams of paperwork entailed to do a transfer, "name, bank, address, blood type, star sign", married to a host of large bank charges and dodgy exchange rates which worked exclusively in the Bank's favour put me right off.

I didn't swear, nor did I didn't transfer over a huge sum of money (all I had) to secure fame in the annals of the Wine Label Circle's Master List. I just gave up, as so many have done before and since, when faced with an unhelpful auctioneer.

It was the next morning, quite depressed by the whole roller-coaster, that a wild thought occurred to me. What if this desperately unhelpful auctioneer had put EVERYONE off bidding, not just me? What if the lot had sold for pences to a local dealer who would have no idea of the treasure he had and bought 40 "bottle tags" he wanted to get rid of, what if? Where would he sell them, perhaps online?

Everyday from then on I started my day by typing "Golden Cordial" into the Ebay search bar more in hope than expectation. Everyday it returned:

"0 results".

It was only three long months later, when pressing a hopeless, hapless ENTER on "search" that the image of two very familiar urn shaped wine labels appeared, in the words of the seller: "white metal bottle tags marked Golden Cordial".

This time it was Ebay and a private seller with no unhelpful auctioneer inbetween demanding 4000 pounds of flesh upfront, this time I could bid online form the comfort of home, albeit at 3.30am in the morning (when the listing ended), in my Pyjama's with a blanket over my head sipping hot chocolate.

Second chances rarely present themselves in the world of antiques so I considered carefully what they were worth, but then decided "sod it" and left everything I could reasonably beg, borrow and steal as my bid, a bit over $3000 at the time (though I believed the labels to be well worth it). I hoped, prayed, none of the very big wine label collectors with bottomless pockets had seen them, I hoped Karma may step in and reward my perseverance in the face of the unhelpful auctioneer, I hoped for a miracle...and...and...

So here it is, though I don't know your name, the biggest thankyou to the very unhelpful auctioneer who refused to take my enormous commission bid in the first place, God Bless You and God Bless America!

I ended up the owner of two of the rarest American silver wine labels (or bottle tags) you'll ever see, Mrs Harriott Pinckney Horry's Golden Cordial from 1770, searched for, fought for, hoped and prayed for and ultimately bought for... £65 (including international postage and customs charges)

Chapter 13: Not my first "Road-eo-Show"

Many years ago, more than a decade but not quite two, before certain people at the BBC had circulated my picture on a Wanted Poster, a series of high level miss-steps and poor executive decisions had led me to be invited along to film on the Antiques Roadshow. Back then I had no idea of what was in store, back then it was the realisation of a childhood dream.

I would appear three times and three times only on "the Roadshow". The same number of times that Peter had been tempted into denying knowing Christ though that had a happier ending, believe me no one was getting resurrected at the end of all this.

The first time I was invited to initially "sit in" alongside the expert in my specialism antique silver, though in this case a "sit in" was not an act of defiance or protest but one of sublimation.

In the unlikely event that things went well, I might be asked to film something for the program itself, something which might even be broadcast. The valuation day was being held in a nearby Cathedral so it was possible that a miracle might happen, more likely there than the local sports centre.

Cathedrals are imposing places full of centuries, even millennia of history. Gothic beauties erected over a hundred years, imposing and breathtaking places for silent contemplation of our Lord who had thrown the money lenders from the temple, so doing mass valuations in the same space for the TV was probably, in a spiritual sense at least, cutting it fine for all concerned. Though was it not written in the Bible that when three or more are gathered in one place for a valuation, I shall be there? Well I was, we all were, not solely for the historic splendour of the back drop, that was only a bonus. We were there because at the time Churches or Cathedrals were the cheapest large spaces to hire out mid-week for filming in the entire of Britain.

I had put on my best suit, it was my only suit so therefore my best. My shoes had been shined so intensely that for a moment the mirror like reflection made it look as if I owned two suits, but it was still just one. The knot on my tie had been adjusted more times than the timing on a Formula One race car and to as little practical effect. Despite this I was not just one, but several bundles of nerves.

The Director or floor manager or perhaps it was the tea boy had asked me to arrive no later than nine o'clock in the morning so I duly turned up at a sprightly ten to seven. I sat as inconspicuously as I could with such reflective footwear in the aisles, quietly watching the entire theatre of "the Roadshow" assemble, I even managed to get a cup of tea (no charge). The day then started in the way the whole of my experience would, oddly and badly.

The silver expert, let's call him "Mr Delivery Van" approached me. I had spoken to him at a lunch at Goldsmiths Hall and then once or twice at Sotheby's in the previous few years, I had even posted some spoons out to him for free. I'm sure he would, if not remember me, know me through the brotherhood of the trade. He extended a friendly hand and began,

"Hello, I was just saying to the Director who is this chap? I mean I just didn't know who you were, I said, yes I said to the Director, WHO IS HE?"

He was at this point still smiling a pleasant smile and shaking my hand vigorously, but continued,

"I mean who is he? I'd never, no, I'd never heard of YOU, never heard of you, I just kept saying WHO IS HE?"

I did not manage to formally introduce myself to him and to this day I would not imagine that he knows who I am. I was sure though that I should never put him in the awkward position of asking me again, lest I went for him with a club or any other heavy implement which might come to hand.

Awed, still quite shy and briefly unable to remember who I was (who was I)? I sat a little back from the green baize valuations table as a very long queue of eager members of the public formed, as my colleague for the day still quietly attempted to work out who I was. To his credit he ushered me to draw close and we began offering valuations to the expectant owners as the queue split in half, on one side those clearly happy to be seeing him, a well known and beloved face off the Telly, the other struggling to cope with the anger and disappointment of having to see me. None asked me to my face who I was, there was no need, it was written in their eyes. If they did not know that was fine, they could ask the expert to my left and he would tell them he did not know either.

The first lady I saw had a big bag of Kings pattern flatware. Being in the presence of a big bag of silver, antique silver, put me instantly at ease like being on autopilot. As she pulled out spoons and forks and laid them before me, I picked them up and sure enough they were by Eley, Fearn and Chawner, all London and all around 1820, but then I noticed something happily odd about the dessert forks.

I turned to the immaculately dressed middle aged owner. Only the best hats and dresses were being worn that day in case fifteen minutes of fame was on the cards. I asked the elaborate hat and the person underneath, supporting it, where the set had come from?

"It's come down the family, it was my Mother's and then I think her Grandfather's"

"Okay" I replied then asked "You don't have any family connections going back to South Africa do you?"

She briefly looked up into the roof space through the brim of the enormous hat, as she pondered, mentally tip-toeing through a lifetimes worth of family stories and recollections,

"My Great Great Grandfather was in the Cape."

That was what I wanted to hear. I lifted up the twelve dessert forks from the set and announced like a Burning Bush with something important to say that they all had hallmarks which looked like London punches but they were in fact pseudo marks struck by Cape silversmiths sometime in the 1820's or 30's, they had either replaced or extended the original London service.

The hat and the person beneath it were clearly both delighted and so was I, I hadn't choked but carried out my first pain free valuation and no one had to be sedated, not even me. In the meantime the expert I was "shadowing", the proper expert (the one that everyone in the queue hadn't paid but wanted to see) had stopped what he had been doing and turned to listen in on my first valuation.

As the hat and it's owner got up and left happy with the new found fragment of family history he tapped me on the shoulder,

"Very interesting that, about the Cape silver forks. You really should have filmed that."

Shit. Of course a miracle had happened in a Cathedral but I hadn't quite been quick enough on the uptake to realise it, I REALLY should have filmed it, but no. As I turned to look at the crowd scanning all the hats for the right one the owner had disappeared from sight. The saddest words of all are these "what might have been". If I'd only remembered to film the forks.

The day progressed well as the hats kept coming, mostly with owners underneath them. I did get to film something, one thing, though not nearly as interesting as the Cape silver forks I had let escape me earlier in the day. Still by the end of it I was feeling as relaxed as any interloper could and ever so slightly more confident, well let's say less unconfident and as a bonus, for a clear two or three hours, no one had asked who I was.

As the day came to a pleasant end and the queue for the silver table all but disappeared members of the Church, who had been hiding out back drinking and playing cards, or administering to the poor and needy, I forget which, appeared en masse with suspiciously full carrier bags of swag.

The Dean of the Cathedral had in particular a family silver bowl he wanted looked at. Very understandably when he came and sat at our table I was never looked at or addressed, he was here for the opinion of the organ grinder not the monkey, I should just sit quietly and eat my nuts.

He passed over a small plain heavy round bowl to the expert (the famous one), who tipped it up in his hands and turned it over, then pulled out a large copy of Jackson's silver hallmarks to turn to the appropriate city and date letter cycle. As he did so he passed the bowl to me so I too could have a look, I flipped it over and almost unconsciously blurted out,

"London, 1738"

The expert didn't look up from his book but just shouted a firm withering "No"

then took it back off me. I could have died on the spot as all my good work seemed to go up in flames. There was another tense pause as I sat fully and deeply in my admonishment.

"No" he repeated as his finger ran down the list of date letters,

"Oh. Yes. Yes you were right, yes it is London 1738"

Immeasurable relief, joy unbounded. Foolishly at that point I thought the hard part was over. I went home happy, I had no idea what was yet to come.

It was about a week later that BBC executives made a second fatal error, fuelled perhaps by too much sugar in the canteens free biscuits and phoned me back, asking me to come along to my second ever Roadshow. This time I was not the monkey but a fully formed organ grinder, no not like that, but as the proper actual silver expert. Delighted at the terrifying honour every preparation it was possible for me to make was made.

My best and only suit would have to be worn for the second time that year so it was sent to the dry cleaners (we never sent things to the dry cleaners), my shoes were particularly shined and a special case, a travel case with wheels and an extending handle was purchased for a full twelve of your British pounds. I had decided ignorance would not be bliss and to take every single book of hallmarks I could conceivably be asked to call into use. This was before the internet was available for random off the cuff (and often useless) research. You only had your brain and your books and I didn't entirely trust the former so would be stocked up with the latter the best I could. I wasn't going to take either of them for granted.

As I was fretting over getting all the books into the extremely heavy travel case, I asked Mum to pack my suit and clothes for the day. I would just travel down in my rough old thick black top and joggers for comfort, only to appear spick and span on the day. Also it was quite hot and the peak of summer and I knew I'd sweat like an Iberico porker heading for the curing room in that boxy little Polo I was driving.

That evening I pulled into the car park of a nearby Travelodge which had the faded glory of a disused nuclear bunker. I latterly heard stories of the bacchanalian excesses of the Roadshow overnights in five star hotels, the drinking sessions which lasted until three or four in the morning and the stories of beds not slept in, sadly these glory days of hedonism were, even then, behind us, I had been born too late for and now it was depressingly all very proper.

I came down to dinner in my scruffy casual clothes, only mistaken twice for one of Travelodge's cleaning staff and began the evening as I meant to go on, with my foot firmly in my mouth. I warmly greeted one of the fellow experts mistaking him for an old Sotheby's colleague, no he was not that man but ran a saleroom, a well known saleroom in that same catchment area and the colleague I'd confused him for was his bitter and sworn rival for every deceased estate in a thirty mile area for the last quarter of a century. He probably thought (and would have been quite justified for thinking) that I was quite deliberately taking the piss.

So the unhappy evening continued with me sitting somehow already relegated to the naughty children's table with all the very most prim and proper of people (not my crowd). When a discussion started on how there were far less Antiques around than thirty years ago I was stupid enough to briefly remove my foot from my mouth again and attempt to join the conversation, a mistake I have not made since.

I pointed out that apart from loss and damage at a very small percentage the same number of antiques existed, indeed in the intervening period pieces from the late nineteenth century had been reclassified from collectables to antiques, so if anything was true it was that there were even more antiques in the World. It only seemed there were less with sadly so many more people chasing them. I was met with silence and angered glares, the observation, though entirely accurate that I had hoped would prove insightful had been a gauntlet across several older faces, it had gone down like a lead balloon.

I bid an early evening farewell then walked, ran, to my small inhospitable room in the cut price bunker themed Travelodge, it was then I undressed and showered and went to arrange my clothes for the next day, having already stuffed all the old ones into the side pockets of my bag.

I hung up the dry cleaned jacket, laid the trousers over the back of the rickety hotel chair pressed my tie flat, pants and socks on the side and shoes on the floor, I reached into my bag to pull out my shirt to air, my hand nervously hit the bare bottom of the leather lining, where was my new forty pound light pink cotton shirt? The answer, of course, was over one hundred and twenty miles away, sitting on the beside cabinet in my home, still awaiting being put into my travel bag.

I won't repeat what I said that evening, I won't

recount the panic I felt. Let's just say I was never a small man so the possibility of borrowing a clean shirt from anyone else was out, unless I borrowed two and was prepared to stitch them together. Travelling back so late in the evening to retrieve my own was impossible and as I had the family car, no one would be driving up with a clean shirt early the next morning.

The choice was simple. If I didn't want to conduct my very first solo valuation day wearing a tie over bare pale exposed breasts and a bulging hairy stomach that no one wanted to see I would have to wear the only shirt that was there and that fitted me, the thick black casual shirt that I had sweated through that day with and stuffed into the pocket of my bag. I teased the unpleasant moistened fabric out and left it up to air as best I could. That night, not since I was a child, I knelt at my bedside and prayed, little knowing that God would hear me, but only think I was joking.

The next morning I dressed. A light grey suit, a purple tie all doing their very best to conceal the thick black soft crumpled shirt I was wearing for the second day in a row on what would turn out to be one of the hottest days of the year, of any year yet recorded. Remember that black absorbs the heat along with shame and regret. The colour combination meant I looked like a low budget slightly overweight UK version of Miami Vice, if there was a gang of international based drug dealers using this valuation day for cover they were certainly in trouble, though it would take a while for me to roll over the bonnet of my car to apprehend them and then there was always the chance that the bonnet could not take the weight.

By breakfast I had resigned myself to having the best day that I could, Columbian based drug cartels not withstanding, and that the missing shirt had done its worst and I was over any further misadventures. I went out to the car with my bag in the boot and the large travel case on wheels full of books beside me and set off for the venue, a large publicly run private house in council grounds, again as a venue insistently cheap to hire for the day.

We had all been given a map of where to park, a small private car park adjacent to the public one and nearer the main building, a parking pass to display in the car and a name badge. I'm not bad with maps and found it with ease, the private car park was indeed right next to the public one and beside a small box hedged garden with coarse gravel pathways in the Elizabethan style.

As I pulled up I was beginning to feel better about the whole day, it was sunny and clear, I was here with my books and all I had to do was settle down at the valuations table and enjoy the day.

I parked easily and took the wheelie case out from the seat beside me, I pulled out the extending handle and as it was very heavy, gripped it firmly and pulled it behind me with a bold determined stride as I walked down the path.

There was a clear line of sight from the public car park to the one I had been in and the gravel path leading down through the box garden to the Hall, so somebody might have seen it happen. If it had been the days when everyone had a mobile phone with them and filmed it you would have seen it happen too, perhaps a million times on YouTube.

If you had been watching you would have seen a fat Miami Vice suited figure pulling a travel case on wheels behind him falling, horizontally, like a stiffened board, out of view behind a two foot high box hedge onto a coarse gravel path. As I had reached the path, roughly tugging the travel case full of heavy books, a jagged piece of gravel must have inserted itself into one of the plastic wheels, locking it dead shut. My tight grip on the handle meant it stopped me in my tracks, hurling me forward and I landed without any warning firmly and fully on the several and sharp upturned points of the gravel, like a Fakir on a bed of nails, I felt like saying Fakir or something similar. Keaton, Buster not Diane, would have been proud.

I was out of it for about a minute, falling so hard I did pass out, but recovered enough to get back up or I would not be telling you the tale now. The palm of my free hand took some of the impact and was bleeding slightly, the other hand, still locked on the bag handle beside me was gently sprained but the real heroes had been my knees that had taken the full and unforgiving force of the impact, they both felt a bit wet.

I stumbled painfully to the valuations table still in a bit of daze and found a chair out of the sun beneath the shade, it was getting very hot and my head was slightly spinning. I managed to discreetly pull the trouser legs up and inspect the damage, I had not landed in a puddle but instead had a healthy amount of blood flowing from each of several punctures to both knee caps. Five minutes of excruciating pressure with two of my three hankies took care to stem the flow. This I felt was as bad as things were ever going to get, it was still half an hour until we "opened" and someone was going to get me a cup of tea, I had asked for four sugars, everything was still going to be FINE.

After about twenty minutes I had settled, got my books out and drank my very sweet tea. I was sharing a table with another expert, in jewellery, let's call him "Mr Bunny" and it would be a nice quiet convivial day, though it was getting hotter, the sun was shining down and I could not take off my jacket without revealing the full horror of the crumpled black shirt I was wearing below. Still I was in the shade and settled. Then "Mr Bunny" arrived, a thin immaculately dressed man in a large panama hat, I smiled and shook his hand, with my lightly sprained not bloody one. His first words were:

"You'll have to move I'm afraid I've very sensitive to the sun and must be in the shade at all times"

I smiled and nodded as if he'd made a little joke, but he was not laughing.

"You'll have to sit over there I'm afraid, I MUST be in the shade" he again insisted in a more deliberate tone.

I did not want to recount my morning of doom and struggled to my feet, my knees now properly in complete agony having both swollen slightly and shifted around the circular table into the full and unremitting glare of the morning Sun, shuffling my books around as I did so. I have since seen footage of "Mr Bunny" filmed at very many outdoor locations, in strong, bright, radiating sunshine. I can only give thanks that his condition is now cured.

Overcooked lobsters were not the colour I was turning as the day progressed, an unexpectedly busy day as it turned out, with the queue for silver unrelenting, as was the Sun. I had to film four or five items that day, as I approached to do the first the camera man said,

"That tie will have to go"

My favourite purple tie, about the only part of my wardrobe to have survived unscathed, apparently had a slight pattern on it which was causing an effect on the film, not to worry though, they kept a spare for just such occasions. I was presented with a tired thin, pencil thin, light blue tie which almost glowed with how revolting it was. Against my thick sweat laden black casual shirt and light grey suit I now had the look of an aspiring East end pimp.

I have since then never forgotten a piece of clothing on any trip and I gave the wheelie case away.

Several weeks later I was standing at a regular weekly table top sale with Mum doing brisk business and one of the program's producers turned up browsing. It should have been a nice "hello, how are you?" but there was an attendant look of horror and surprise as she spied me taking a few hundred pounds for a selection of fine Irish bright cut tablespoons,

"Er, you, are you standing...HERE?" she said with a slight air of disgust.

I was a bit taken aback but with a handful of notes in one hand and a bag of spoons in the other I couldn't really duck for cover under my six foot cloth covered trestle table, besides I didn't think there was anything wrong with an antiques dealer dealing, after all that's what antiques dealers do (and some of the best in the business do it from behind a six foot trestle table).

"Yes this is one of my regular fairs"

I suppose, from the worsening look on her face and the way she quickly ran away I could have said, "No I'm just helping out here briefly before going on to my factory which skewers and grinds unwanted orphans into reasonably priced mincemeat" and got the same response. After that I was only ever to get one more call from the Roadshow and that was in desperate times indeed.

The following year, after being dropped quicker than a hot, poor, antiques fair-going potato, the phone rang and I was asked if I could "fill in" for a valuation day in London. The expert who was meant to be attending had been knocked off his motorcycle by a car and broken his arm or leg (no I wasn't driving, I wouldn't have missed). This was indeed a novel occurrence as most arms and legs that get broken in the antiques trade are done so around "financial restructuring arrangements", by blokes called "Dave".

I knew I had been put out to dry but thought it churlish and petty to refuse, they were in a jam and besides they would also pay me, so I would be there the next day to just lend a hand (I would not overnight) and this time it would be just me and my pocket Jacksons, without a wheelie case in sight.

The valuation day was being held at the last travelling steam fair, it was all rather bright and garish and the day started well, no one fell over and both knees were blood free and moving. Lots of people turned up but with pretty uninspiring items.

London was a well worn area and anything of any real value or interest was either locked away in a penthouse safe or already in Sotheby's warehouse waiting to be lotted and sold. One dear old lady nearly gave me a heart attack when she pulled out of a bag a silver monument candlestick which was finer than the pair Mrs How had bought for the Aga Khan years earlier for over a hundred thousand pounds, but a quick examination showed it to be Victorian electroplate copy. Then a gentleman appeared with a small bear pin cushion with moveable arms and legs, it was quite rare and a colleague had, I knew, just sold one for an enormous sum of money, I put it forward to be filmed.

It was going to be a quick piece, no more than a minute or so, in out and a reaction, fine. I had to find a line to start the conversation, by then asking "how did you come by it?" was getting hackneyed but I thought I had the perfect intro,

"So are you an Arctophile?"

The man looked both shocked and offended, when I asked. Wait what was it, yes a word ending in "phile" had he misheard? I quickly went on and reassured him,

"No don't worry its not anything sinister, it just means a Teddy Bear collector"

I quickly ran through the description and finished, had that really just happened? Well it still went out, slight brief horrified reaction and all, but this was a long time ago remember, when Jim, at the BBC at least, was still allowed to Fix It.

The day, my last ever day on the Roadshow ended as badly as it possibly could. A lady had brought in a stupendously vile Britannia metal jug and perhaps because antiques on the day had been thinner on the ground than a slice of Melba toast, the Director wanted to film it. But he wanted to film it on the "Pirate Ship".

I am terrified of heights. Not particularly how high up you are but how precarious you might be. The "Pirate Ship" was a wooden swinging boat about twenty or thirty feet up in the air. You walked up a thin unsteady staircase to get on it and there was a gap between you and the boat of around a foot which you stepped over, there was no guard and the ground below, way below, was clearly visible…and the boat swung as you stepped on. I tried everything except for admitting my terror to get out of it, no dice.

I felt sick, nearly was sick, but managed to get up the stairs with slender insubstantial rail clasped white knuckle tight in my hand. I was swaying a bit but not as much as the Pirate Ship.

Camera crew and sound men leapt over, they were gazelle like, though I have never been compared to one. It took five men to hold the ship for me just to get into this wooden cradle of death. I was genuinely terrified and the valuation I gave proved it. I simply could not think beyond the delight of being safely on the ground again, it may have been the quickest valuation in Roadshow history.

So was I sad to say farewell? No not really, someone "up there" had decided from the off it was not for me and they had been trying to tell me something I'd steadfastly refused to hear.

I'd also observed the great unspoken truth that if you stand with feet of clay in front of cameras, lights and often undeserving public adoration, those same weak insubstantial feet can bake hard under the glare and you risked forgetting that your feet were clay at all, mistaking that hard baked clay for stone.

My luck had been in all my various misfortunes, my luck though I did not know it back then had been to get out in time, even though I'd been pushed.

Happily I returned to other programs, simpler ones, without pretence or ambition, full of fun, friends and laughter under lights which would never glare so bright or terrify, ones without a Pirate Ship or hedged gravel path anywhere in sight.

Chapter 14: Revenge is a dish...

Never for a moment think the world of antiques isn't strewn with pitfalls and bear traps. Anyone who tells you they've never fallen into one is either lying or unable to feel the teeth of the trap biting into their lower leg, probably because of nerve damage, and some of these people have a lot of nerve.

One particularly bitter experience was being, in local parlance "legged over" by a local jeweller who I later learnt had the scruples of Machiavelli and the charm of Hitler. It was, however, as most of these things are, entirely my own fault. I had taken to visiting shops and dealers trying to sell them my wares directly. This particular jeweller smelt blood in the water when I showed him a fine Irish silver cream jug and a Victorian silver mustard pot, which I was hoping to make a small margin on.

"Well, I've got this lovely silver teapot if you're interested?"

I was. Swapping a silver jug and mustard pot for a silver teapot seemed more than fair and if it had been a silver teapot it would have been.

"It's got some odd marks on the bottom, but a lovely piece" he continued.

They were, I was later to find out, indeed odd marks for a piece of silver but not for a piece of Victorian electroplate. You may argue I should have known what I was doing (and you're right) but it was all still new to me as I was only a teenager. He had cheated a schoolboy out of his savings, but someone was probably going to anyway and the lesson it served up, hard to swallow, was a valuable one and perhaps worth the price of those two pieces of silver.

Many years passed and I had all but forgotten the incident of the electroplated teapot, though not entirely. The jeweller in question had understandably gone from strength to strength, owning racehorses, even advertising on local television trying to corner the "schoolboy with silver Irish cream jugs to sell" side of the market (it was after all, very lucrative).

I'd grown considerably in that time, not just sideways but with knowledge, Sotheby's had taught me a lot and I was even starting to appear on TV myself as an "Antiques Expert". Unfortunately, Sotheby's hadn't paid well and the BBC seemed to be paying me in used crisp packets rather than actual money so I had to ply my trade on the streets. I had not become a male escort you understand, nothing quite so noble, I was a near penniless antiques dealer.

One thing that had happened in the meantime was that both gold and silver had started to climb up in price as a commodity. The news spread and soon little old ladies, up and down the country, were clambering through their dressers, trunks and attics for anything displaying the merest of metallic gleams to hurry along and exchange a century of family sentiment for cold hard cash. I knew from experience that often the high street jeweller was the first port of call (not the antiques dealer or auctioneer) when it came to selling "scrap" so determined to go round all the local jewellers to see if they had bought anything interesting, and when I say all the local jewellers I included the one who had "legged me over" all those years ago.

It had been a pretty fruitless day by the time I arrived at HIS shop. The public had been mostly scrapping 9ct gold (utterly without) charm bracelets, signet rings and quite worryingly I did see a couple of teeth, though happily no pliers were on view and no blood was dripping from them. "Still must do them all", I thought as I opened the Victorian glazed door at the front of the shop as the shrill insistent bell alerted all to my presence.

"Hello, just wondered if you had any odd boxes of antique scrap silver I could look through?"

A figure, plump, almost bursting with profit, like a well fed Hobbit appeared, silver coiffeured hair and immaculately dressed.

"I've got a box of spoons here you can look through if you want"

The tone was slightly dismissive, he knew I was "in the trade" and not likely to ever pay any of the ticket prices which were on display, most of which could have all been written by Tolkein, given they were such monumental works of fiction.

The box was fetched from the back room and dropped unceremoniously in the deepest darkest corner of the small shop, so I would be in no position to disturb an actual proper "victim"(customer). It all seemed a bit grubby and I thought for a second to leave, but how could I with an unsearched box of silver spoons before me?

My hands delved in, sorting and sifting through spoon after spoon, breaking the still oppressive quiet of the shop with the soft pitch tumbling of silver stem onto silver stem, then bowl.

They were all crap.

That is to say a collection of uninteresting, mass produced Fiddle pattern spoons from the nineteenth century, all made in London or Sheffield, all terribly boring, crap. That was until a crest, an early crest on the back of a spoon poked through, I hurriedly pulled it out. It was a different pattern, an earlier pattern to the rest, Hanoverian. The stem was elegant and curved upwards. The spoon itself was all hand raised and the crest of a Crowned Head was simply beautiful, but the marks were pinched closed, still I put it in my other hand and looked further into the box only to find its matching pair a moment later, just the same, but this time the hallmarks had been clearly, beautifully struck and I knew immediately what they were. Steady, I thought.

"Er, Hi, Hello, these two here, how much have you got on them?" I asked as casually as I possibly could under the circumstances.

"Hmmm" his eyes darted towards me and a look of complete alarm and suspicion fell over his face now I'd actually found something I wanted to buy. It was the same look that Gollum gave Bilbo when he tried to have it away with his ring.

"Let's see"

He rested the spoons from my hands with a single swift grasp.

"What are the hallmarks? London?" he queried out loud.

"I, I don't know without looking them up (I lied) but the Crests are nice, I like the Crests"

Whilst I was speaking he'd turned and got out his large tattered copy of Jacksons (the bible of English silver marks) and started running through the pages to find the mark.

"Oh yes, here, here it is, London, London 1720 (I did not correct him) oh they're early" a tone of greed and satisfaction entered his voice "Yes a nice early pair of spoons these"

"So how much?"

He paused and then became brusk.

"I don't know, I'll have to do a bit of research, you'll have to go now I'm busy" though the shop was pin drop quiet and as empty as any politician's head.

"Well you did say the spoons were for sale" I timidly insisted.

"Yes, yes I know and they are but you'll have to come back, come back next week and I'll have a price for you then"

"Okay, I'll pop back next week" I said, utterly disheartened.

As I spoke I was being ushered from the shop by the deeply unpleasant jeweller.

The week passed and my impatience grew as my expectations diminished. It's now that I should tell you what the spoons actually were. They weren't London at all but from the much rarer Assay Office of York, though if you don't know what you're doing it is possible to confuse a fairly commonplace "London 1720" with an extremely rare "York 1780" which is exactly what he had done.

I went back a week later fully expecting two things, firstly he would out of a sheer force of greed have found out what the spoons were, secondly he would want a King's ransom for them. If that was so I'd determined to buy the good spoon with the clear marks and leave the second. I entered the shop.

"Morning, I've come..."

"About the spoons, yes" He smiled smugly, my heart sank.

"Yes I was right on the day but you understand I have to double check these things, a nice early London pair of spoons"

"So, er, have you got a price?"

"Yes £180 for the pair"

I should say that wasn't a dear price but neither I thought was it dirt cheap and, still being paid in used crisp packets by the BBC, every penny counted.

"Well I really only wanted the one with the good marks, could I just give you £140 for that?"

I had clearly angered Gollum with the offer.

"It's ONE EIGHTY THE PAIR!"

"What about £160 for the good one?" I bravely, foolishly replied.

"No, THE PAIR OR NOTHING!"

I quickly gave up and paid him for the spoons. I

wanted them and had still done well, besides I could always sell the other one for £20, if anyone would have it with such pinched marks, and get my money back that way, it was just a bit more hassle. I thanked him and left.

When I got home I admired the spoons, they were both lovely, should I split them up? But I had been prepared to walk away with just one and even £20 was a serious amount of money to me at the time.

I'd only really just started selling things on EBay, it was a minefield full of nutters (sorry, discerning but thrifty collectors), but it seemed the easiest thing to do. I'd list the spoon with the poorer marks for 99p and hope it made me £20 or maybe even £30 back? It wasn't long after the listing went live I started to get a flurry of questions about the spoon, "how did I know it was York not London?", "Where did it come from?" quite brusk in tone, the correspondent didn't give a name. I looked at the user Id. It wasn't a name either, just a series of numbers and three letters at the end, the letters were by great coincidence the initials of the Jeweller I had just bought it from and this user was selling himself on Ebay, lots and lots of jewellery and he was located in my home city.

This was perhaps revenge enough, not that he hadn't made money, I'm sure he had. But I felt very "Darth

Vadar" about the whole thing, I had known more than he had, I'd passed him and left him standing and what's more he now knew it through his EBay inquiries. I was waving a bright red light sabre around and he was a pile of Tatooine robes on the floor. This was enough, enough to make up for that young boy's electroplated "silver" teapot, but there was one little bit more to come.

The spoons were rarer than I had thought, the pattern, Hanoverian, had only been made for a few short years at York, so even this later example was really very rare. The spoon I'd offered, begged not to take, the poor one that he was watching me sell online, the one he'd insisted I buy just so he could get that extra £20 for himself, it sold for a little over £200. In a single blow all my money back and the spoon I had wanted all along, for free, a debt of more than a decade swiftly and justly repaid.

Now, I know that the saying we are all familiar with is slightly wrong, there's an error and it's just one letter, so let me correct it and assure you from true and honest experience that revenge is a dish best served...OLD!

Chapter 15: A pleasure to see you

Nowadays I'm rarely parted from the sofa as I bid online, sitting comfortably with the dog asleep against my leg and an endless supply of hot tea and biscuits in front of me. Go back ten, fifteen years and it was a different picture, popping in the car and dashing around the country to view sale after sale, picking through hundreds of boxes of rubbish for just a glimpse of a gem.

I'll say now that as an auctioneer I very much enjoyed conducting a sale but as a dealer I've never really enjoyed having to sit through an entire one.

Prior to the internet I would spend 50% of my working life driving hundreds of miles (a week) in an unreliable beaten up car, 49% of my time sitting in a saleroom watching lots that I had absolutely no interest in sell and only 1% actually bidding and then trying to sell whatever I managed to buy. That's probably not quite true but it certainly felt like it.

When you drive to auctions rather than have the luxury of scrolling through a catalogue online you simply can't go everywhere. That inescapable fact sustained the dealing side of the trade for the better part of a couple of hundred years before modern technology reared its head.

Every dealer worked their "patch", though I was less disciplined, a maverick who could pop up almost anywhere I felt a good sale was being held. It was when I was young and had the energy, regarding the 100 mph mark on the speedometer of my decrepit red Mini Metro, to be an implied minimum rather than an absolute maximum (and yes, it eventually did blow up).

I was never a known "regular" at any particular saleroom, so my presence was almost always greeted with at best curiosity and at worst suspicion from the other dealers, "why is he here?"

A couple of auctions stand out in my memory. First a sale where a fantastically rare Elizabethan silver dish had turned up. I'd been having sleepless nights about it for a couple of days given its age, extreme rarity and the saleroom estimate, which when all things were considered, was somewhat modest being only £20-40.

On the day of the auction I bought it against the local trade for let's say "a good deal more" but that's not the point of this tale. Upon getting back home from the auction late that evening the phone rang. It was a dealer I knew who lived a few hours away who I hadn't seen for a while and almost never telephoned me.

"Hello, have you been out and about bidding today?"

"Yes, why do you ask?"

"Oh I've a mate who's fuming. He tried to buy this little silver dish today in a sale but was outbid. He didn't know who it was that bought it, just told me it was a big (euphemism for fat) bloke with glasses and a red beard. I just wondered...?"

My cover was blown. It's a small world and I was now and possibly forever the "fat bearded bloke with the glasses", though in later years and with a deal of acrimony from some of the more established silver trade, the "bloke" part was often substituted with something shorter, something pithier, something Anglo Saxon.

Though my most memorable (and well timed) encounter occurred some time after that. A now well known celebrity auctioneer (let's call him Carlos) was just starting up by selling out of a local hotel.

His first few sales were, like many of the catalogue descriptions, hit and miss. Though in the sale I went to there appeared to be quite a lot of silver.

Having driven down early, parked up and entered a Middle England version of the Bates Motel, I descended to the downstairs "suite". It was a thickly, busily, carpeted area, a poorly lit lounge which surely, at weekends, bore witness to some of the unhappiest wedding receptions in the Country.

Despite the whole floor being given over to the days proceedings it was a desperately tight fit. Auction lots, cabinets, staff, bidders, a portable rostrum (Auction not Swordfish), rows of chairs, etc had to be shoe horned in. You edged around the entire sale uttering "excuse me" like a low Benedictine chant and gently squeezed or nudged your way around the display cases as elderly ladies, bound only for a day out, stood nattering with a steadfast determination to remain unmoved.

After a deal of manoeuvring I eventually reached the silver section and was open mouthed at the number of lots along with the spectacular inaccuracy of the cataloguing that accompanied them.

First in my sights were a set of "white metal plates" valued slightly under their scrap price as they were only "low grade continental silver". In fact I was holding three graduated dishes marked for one of the Swiss cantons and dating back to the later part of the eighteenth century, each with a fine family armorial to the edge. I won't list it all now but there was a wealth of early European and English Silver there that day, tureens, teapots, mugs, cups, bags and bags stuffed with French and Swiss eighteenth century flatware. Even then I knew it was going to be a bloodbath and I would have to pick my moment to have any chance of success.

One lot in particular stood out to me. It was simply catalogued as a "metal goblet £40-60". Why I don't know as it was fully and clearly marked for Dublin 1798 under the foot, though that wasn't even the best part. The best part was it had a lengthy period inscription commemorating the 1798 Irish rebellion and toasting all those involved on the Irish side, I'd never seen such a historically important piece of Irish Georgian silver before.

I settled down for the long haul and bagged an end of row chair before they were all taken, many already had coats draped over their backs as "beach towel markers". The auctioneer, who I knew, passed nearby and we exchanged a brief but cheery "hello" amid the morning throng, as dealers chitchat moved up from a murmur to a deafening chorus, only to be cut short in its tracks by the sharp sound of a gavel hitting the wooden block three times in quick succession, signalling the auction was about to start.

The silver, happily, was the first section in the sale so I wouldn't be there all day. The Swiss meat dishes made well over their estimate (but still beyond my pocket with the Irish goblet firmly in my sights). Though the group of silver dealers I knew crowded around the rostrum were still all broadly smiling as the hammer fell. You could say a good day was going to be had by all, with the possible exception of the vendor.

An hour passed and I may have bid on a couple of cheaper things (probably spoons) but I was steadfastly determined to give the goblet my very best shot.

The time came. The auctioneer, oblivious to the rarity of the item he was selling, leaned over the intimate crowd of prospective bidders with arms flailing in the air and started the bidding off at £40. One of the silver dealers next to the rostrum feigned disinterest and whilst half looking away whispered

"Yes Sir."

There was a pause and everyone else seemed disinterested, the hammer began to fall as my hand rose and I added my own, more emphatic "Yes Sir" to the chorus, "and fifty now" called out the auctioneer as he pointed towards me with that ominous small wooden hammer.

The other dealer was immediately disgruntled, looking like a wolf who thought he'd caught a lamb only to see it slip free and begin to run, the chase was on. We went back and forth continuously in agonising ten pound increments all the way to seven hundred pounds. By the time the hammer fell, in my favour, most of the seated pensioners in the saleroom had woken up due to the commotion and the auctioneer was positively grinning and gesticulating more than usual from the lively bidding conflict.

I rose quickly to leave but had to push through the other bidders, past the rostrum to ascend the thickly, vividly carpeted stairs. As I squeezed by, the auctioneer, delighted by the result and still writing my number down in the auction book declared for all to hear:

"It's always a pleasure to see you..."

as the dealer I had just outbid, standing below but also directly beside the rostrum loudly added, as quick as a flash and without a moment's hesitation:

"...no it fucking isn't."

The room erupted with laughter. It was peerless comic timing. About five minutes later the same dealer, who I knew, came up to me in the queue for accounts, full of apology but told me he simply couldn't resist the opportunity and had hoped he hadn't offended me. Far from it I was still chuckling about it, but then I had also won my prize.

And the goblet? Well that really was rarer than a hens tooth. I foolishly sold it for a small wheelbarrow full of cash some time later when I really should have gotten a large one for it. It went to a good home and returned to Ireland, where it should have been all along.

The auction itself wouldn't happen in the same way these days. Everything would be streamlined, automated, online and ruthlessly efficient with bids coming in from across the globe. You won't have to dislodge any old ladies from beside cabinets with forceful thrusts of your elbows or take a good half hour to push past everyone in doing a single circuit of the saleroom. In truth you probably wouldn't even be there to view or bid.

Still, I won't complain, the "brave new auction world" suits me very well now, though I may think back fondly to the days when it was always "a pleasure to see you".

Chapter 16: The Merry-Go-Round

Every month or so, back when unleaded petrol was only sixty pence a litre, I would regularly visit friends in London. Being a "dealer" in the loosest sense of the word meant that whenever I was around for the weekend I felt obliged to call in to Portobello road.

Happily the movies never got it right. No cheery salt of the earth Londoners were singing whilst executing minutely choreographed routines up the length of the road, nor were fopish casually attired ex Etonians bumping into incognito movie stars, no it was all more gloriously mercenary than that.

As the outside stalls set up and awnings over the indoor markets were pulled out, I headed off to pay homage to that famous impish scholar of Indian Colonial silver. He stood always wearing an apron behind the counter of his stall, master of a hundred little boxes of miscellaneously hallmarked oddities, some of which you might be shown, some of which you might not, there was a pecking order, (I was near the bottom and remain there still).

As I rounded the corner to approach I was struck by the site of him, and several other well known silver dealers all crowding around a smaller stand, a little way along from his, as a young dealer (let's call him "donut") arrived and took a bag off his shoulder. As "donut" unzipped it and began to remove carefully wrapped items, a flurry of venerable hands thrust in to pick each of them up. Standing back I watched this feeding frenzy last about ten minutes before the crowd dispersed, with cheery dealers walking away, smiling and chatting to one another all firmly clutching their prizes in their coat pockets.

I approached the little stall to inspect the remnants, the "bones" of that days carcass. I must have motioned with my eyes to the dealer as if to say "what was that all about?" As the reply to what I was thinking came unbidden.

"Yes, you've got to get here early" donut exclaimed. "I travel all over the country each week, I pick up some pretty rare pieces in all sorts of places and only sell them here on Saturday, they all wait for me."

"Oh" I nodded and smiled as I wondered, disappointedly, at what treasures I might have missed.

"It would be worth getting here early next week, around seven, if you're really interested that is" donut's sales pitch continued. I immediately fell for it and assured him I'd be there next week, all the earlier to inspect his Aladdin's Cave of treasures. It would have to be a horribly early start all the way from Birmingham and a good two hour drive, but as I said this was a long time ago and petrol was only sixty pence a litre.

During the week I darted around the country myself. At the time it felt a bit like work but now I would regard it as unabated fun. Each morning I'd choose where I wanted to go (usually an auction viewing) then I had all day to amble back stopping off at any shop or antiques centre I passed for a rummage. I stopped at one shop in a sleepy Oxfordshire village which exclusively sold silver, though there was quite a lot of modern stuff in the window.

Despite the unprepossessing window display I called in and said my "hellos", browsing through the quite pricey stock and engaging the shop owner in intelligent enough conversation so that he would know I was "in the trade". Inevitably I got around to asking THE question you ask in any shop or centre, had he "got anything out the back?". You always hoped there would be oddments which may have just come in from a local private seller or problem pieces the shop owner was unsure of. A knowing "ahh" came as the reply, as he shuffled off into the back room to reappear moments later holding a small wooden tray.

"Some interesting pieces in here, though not for the shop" he said, placing the contents of the tray before me. A handful of worn Georgian teaspoons, a couple of pairs of bright cut sugar tongs and a Hanoverian pattern tablespoon made up the sparse and depressing contents.

The tablespoon was the most interesting. It only had a single maker's mark to the reverse which I recognised as being a Channel Islands silversmith. The mark was nice and clear but sadly a good third of the spoon's bowl had been worn clean away by a couple of hundred years of daily use. Still, I asked the price, it might after all, in this poor condition, cost very little. The reply came back, it didn't.

I left the shop empty handed, it was all a bit thin that week, but still I had the major event lying ahead of me, my Saturday morning Portobello rendezvous, where I hoped a wealth of unseen treasures would be lain before me if I was early enough.

Saturday morning, horribly early on Saturday morning, I pootled down the M40 in the cold darkness, arriving and parking up in a side street at Portobello well before the Sun had arisen. A polystyrene cup of coffee was a necessary extravagance, though the additional four pounds asked for a single warm sausage roll which might have accompanied it was a bridge too far, even though I could happily have eaten ten.

Some milling around the outside stalls proved a way to kill time before heading down to the stall I'd been at a week earlier, though this time I stood waiting ahead of the crowd. The familiar faces of established dealers started to turn up and gather round. Many were perturbed to spy an interloper to these early morning proceedings, but no force on Earth was going to move me from my prime position, I'd been waiting all week for this.

Time dragged on waiting for "donut" to turn up with his knapsack of hidden treasures casually slung over his shoulder. It felt like an eternity, though it was probably no more than ten or fifteen minutes. Eventually he arrived and unzipped open the much anticipated bag of swag. The dealers behind me began jostling and pushing, each wanting first look at the prizes on offer. A box was opened and the young dealer looked pleased with the offertory pile of treasures he placed before us. I looked on in disbelief to see a handful of worn Georgian teaspoons, a couple of pairs of bright cut sugar tongs and a Hanoverian pattern tablespoon with a third of the bowl missing, all eerily familiar.

I stepped back and let the dealers behind me push in and feast on the rotting carcass of a tray of items I'd seen three days earlier in an Oxfordshire village and run away from at half of what was now the asking price. One dealer picked up the horribly worn tablespoon and waving it in the air, taunted another who had just missed out "It's Channel Islands!" he grinned, oblivious it seemed to the appalling condition of it.

I'd witnessed first hand the merry go round of the trade, someone else's rubbish being another's treasure and the overwhelming power of "presentation". A bag full of tat, if anticipated, if being sold as an unseen treasure (that you were lucky enough to be allowed to get first look at), could be happily snapped up by the otherwise most learned and educated of buyers. I thought to learn a valuable lesson that day, driving back home from Portobello, even though I had ended my trip by spending a commiseratory eight pounds for two quite unspectacular and barely warm sausage rolls. Maybe I still had a few more lessons still to learn. Always taking a packed lunch certainly being one of them.

Chapter 17: V for Vendetta and Vetting

Vetting occurs when, irrespective of an antiques fairs size, it becomes "prestigious" either a high profile or a high net worth event, probably both. I'd like to know who first came up with the idea of vetting so if they aren't already dead I can kill them. No, just joking, I KNOW they're dead. I double checked.

The principal was a sound one to begin with. A group of qualified specialists would comb through every dealer's stock to assess that the items offered for sale to an unsuspecting public were genuine, that any restoration was clearly labelled and well done and the last criteria (which has often caused the most trouble) was "fair worthy". This was all carried out so the standards of an event could be maintained and buyers could shop with confidence. All seems like a good idea so far. However what in theory should be a first class bit of consumer protection turns, in practice, to be an exploration of greed, envy, stupidity and duplicity, a vehicle to carry out vendetta within the antiques trade.

I was at a "good regional fair". I'd done it many times before and was used to "Vetting day". The order of business was to set up your stand the day before with the next day spent with the vetters going through a long printed form attached to your stand which covered each and every discipline in the World of Antiques, "silver, furniture, jewellery, treen, English porcelain, etc" no stone was left unturned or unpriced.

A small "mob" of experts would come round and squirrel through all your stock, and here's the first flaw in the system. It was very expensive and laborious to bring in impartial qualified outside experts, so almost all the vetters were other dealers exhibiting at the same fair. What was that? Did somebody say conflict of interest?

In truth, Vetting day was always my best day. Vetters didn't just do the job for the prestige or a complimentary lunch, they came with pockets bulging with cash, cards and cheque books anticipating first dibs, perfectly and greedily placed to take full advantage of it.

A year earlier I'd taken along two rare salt marrow spoons, small silver condiment spoons whose handles were formed as long narrow scoops for bone marrow, to the fair.

"They'll have to come off" said the Head of the

vetting committee (back then a leading silver dealer, nowadays in a witness protection scheme or on the run).

"Why?" I replied

"They stems have been altered into marrow scoops"

I had in truth been well prepared for this to happen given how very unusual and uncommon they were.

I instantly replied: "But they're 1805, so would have been top marked like all flatware of that period, but you can see that they've deliberately struck the marks at the bottom of the stem to accommodate the scoop ends"

There was a slight look of surprise as he gathered himself, Muhammad Ali was very briefly on the mat, I'd "Coopered" him.

"Okay, I'll let you have that one"

Very kind. I was, after pointing it out, allowed to sell a genuine rare antique as a genuine rare antique, where would this magnanimity end? But this is how vetting went, it was opinion against opinion, silverback against silverback. It was war.

This particular year I had my superb coffee pot, some lovely heavy salt cellars, a pristine Georgian tea caddy which was the star of the show and, oh yes a porringer which was a little bit tired.

Every dealer will begin to obsess on Vetting Day that the mob of hungry, feral vetters, eager to justify their existence, will pick out one particular object on your stand and brand it "unfairworthy", tearing it apart with their smiling teeth. This year my little Georgian porringer, that had done no harm to anyone definitely looked the prime candidate for evisceration.

It was sometimes not beyond the guile of older dealers to deliberately bring along one absolute stinker of an object to a fair for precisely this reason, to take the criticisms and abuse, to act as cover. Such ingenuity in the face of arbitary bureaucracy gives one a warm glow, but back then I wasn't quite that sharp, I'm still not.

I had to leave the stand briefly and came back to my stalwart Mother, assistant at all and any fair I ever did, telling me that the vetting committee wanted to see me about one item, ahh, I thought my dear little porringer.

"What do you mean the TEA CADDY?! That's MINT?!!" I wailed in disbelief as my Mother explained.

I was utterly gob smacked. The Tea Caddy was George III, oval drum shaped with a small folding ring handle, everything on it, every surface had the most superb crisp bright cut engraving and a huge coat of arms, it was pin sharp and I genuinely thought the very best piece I'd bought for ages.

One of the vetters (who completely avoided eye contact with me and simply muttered his concerns furtively to another member of the committee) was "worried" about the cover. Hmmm.

"What about the cover?" I said in a quite embattled manner, ready for a fight.

The Head of the vetters, was brought in to take a look (different to the year prior and still very much to his credit not yet on the run). After much umming and ahhing it was decided that the folding ring handle (foolishly shaped for a human finger) should, if of the period, be oval in keeping with the shape of the Caddy (making it utterly weak and unable to accommodate any human finger comfortably). I also pointed out that the engraving went all the way over where it was attached and showed no signs of disturbance. It's now that I should say a Vetting

Committee's decision, when they put their foot down in any fair, is law. My reasoned thinking fell, this time, on deaf ears. I had to label it as with a "later handle" if I wanted to display it, well I might as well go over it with a steam roller as do that.

When they left I asked the "Y's" to look at it. "Y's" are dealers so old and familiar within the trade that you knew them by their first name only, a name which almost always ended with a "Y". They were in fact "the two Y's men".

"What's wrong with that?" I asked the Terry and Kenny, two old men with the combined age of Methuselah and the wisdom of Solomon.

"It's really very nice" said Kenny.

"So there's nothing wrong with it?" I replied

"No, who said there was?" said Terry.

"The Vetting Committee"

"Oh" they both exchanged knowing glances, "You mean the World's leading experts in fuck all!"

They had seen it all before and simply smiled and laughed and, after a while, I did too, though more with relief as at least I wasn't actually losing my marbles and the Caddy was as good as I thought it was.

It confirmed this was a game of favourites and friends, if you go to buy antiques ANYWHERE, wether it's a vetted environment or not, do so by that dealer's individual reputation and not by what onlookers, many with vested or biased interests, are shouting from the stands and shouting with no offer of personal liability or guarantee.

But what became of the maligned Georgian silver Tea Caddy you ask? After the fair (I certainly did not put the Caddy out saying it had the wrong handle) two things happened. Firstly I learnt the small man vetting who never addressed me directly was exhibiting at the fair too. He had a "big client", I was later told, coming specifically to the fair to buy a good Georgian silver Tea Caddy. His buyer may well have left with a good one too, but certainly not the best, I still had that locked away.

The second was one of the older dealers, the "Y's", had a particularly good fair and so bought the Caddy from me as I was packing up on the last day. He sold it on almost immediately for almost twice what he

paid and what's more I was to see it again. A month
or two later it appeared as the headline featured item
in a very prestigious and well known silver dealers
stock at a major international fair, after it had
undoubtedly passed their rigorous vetting process
with flying colours.

Chapter 18: A bit of plastic

When it came to spending money, actual folding cold hard cash on antiques, it took a long time for anyone in my family to have any confidence that I knew what I was doing. Rightly so it must be said. Truthfully it did take me a very long time even to begin to know what I was doing and I suppose I'm still not there yet.

Anyway, even after working at Phillips, then Christie's and finally Sotheby's as a department head, my Mum could still be awfully sceptical and scathing about some of my more "offbeat" purchases.

One day I called into Warwick, visiting all the familiar shops and centres. I kept being drawn back there by odd little finds which would turn up in a pre-internet age. The very best had been a "Victorian patch box" handed out to me from behind a locked glazed cabinet with a ticket price of £25. It was formed as two solid carved pieces of cartouche shaped hardstone, an attractive and rare "puddingstone" with chased foliate gilt metal mounts. Made in Saxony around 1730, I skipped out of the shop with it for all of £20, a minor miracle. That was the drug that had me calling back to Warwick and scouring the shops every few weeks. On this occasion there had been nothing of note until browsing in one of the last cabinets in the largest of the centres right in the middle of town.

Inconspicuously a small boringly brown fob seal lay amongst a tray of oddments. Still, I asked to see it and was surprised to find it was carved out of box or fruitwood. It was the identical form to all the silver fob seals I'd ever seen. The flat oval base was carved with foliate script initials and the tapering faceted stem had two initials "C.C" stamped into the surface. Different from the initials to the base they were almost certainly those of the carver. The ticket price was forty something pounds. I paused and thought for a moment if I could recall ever seeing one carved out of wood, and I couldn't. A few minutes of haggling and the light brown wooden fob seal was mine for £35. It was the sort of odd tactile bit that you constantly wanted to handle, I strolled back to the car park happily toying with it in my hand.

Arriving back home I would always kick off my shoes, pour myself a long cool drink and pile any and all "treasures" on the kitchen table for Mum to inspect and hopefully admire. This day's haul was just the little Georgian fob seal.

"What's this? A bit of plastic?" Mum picked up the seal from the table with a slight air of 'what has he bought now?'

"It's boxwood, or fruitwood a little Georgian seal, circa 1770" I replied.

Mum looked unconvinced and tapped it on our sturdy melamine 1970's dining table to elicit a high pitched "ting".

"That sounds like plastic to me".

I took it in my hands and replied, slightly wounded by the inference,

"No it's wood! Look, it's clearly wood" though I had, momentarily, started to doubt myself. It wasn't made of plastic after all, was it? Some cunning Far Eastern, injection moulded imposter?

This highlighted, even after a decade or more working in Antiques, my substantial insecurities as to my own abilities. On balance such uncertainty is no bad thing. Not when you see how many Muggins are out there making a nefarious living knowing very, very little indeed, skating on thin ice. No, a constant sense of self doubt followed by double, then triple checking everything , that's the key in antiques.

Throughout the day, having sat peering at the seal like a Chimp looking at a smart phone without the instructions, I had firmly convinced myself that it was indeed wood. No matter how many times I tried to argue my corner, pointing out the merest hint of graining, or a build up of dark waxy colour through handling, Mum would remain unconvinced. Tapping it once more against any hard surface and being assured it was a bit of plastic. Determined to prove my point I posted it off to an old college friend.

Years earlier my chum had introduced me to all things wooden and metalwork-y in the world of antiques. A few of us had shared a house together at college and it was here that I first encountered two great antiques reference works in his sparse library, Pinto on Treen and Gentle on Metalwork. Still the standard works many decades later.

Edward Pinto had passed on as had Rupert Gentle, though his wife Belinda was still a stalwart, a pillar of the traditional antiques trade at the time. My friend, a few years older and more enterprising than I, had sought her out, befriending and then selling her a few odds and ends as a "runner".

One lucky day whilst still at College we got the invite to her Grade II listed country house, a visit I was in awe of, but far too young and ignorant to fully appreciate. What a house and what wonderful things inside it! Still the visit had cemented a relationship and set in place a chain of supply. Whenever I found suitably interesting odds and ends on my travels, I'd send them down to my old college friend who would, in turn, add a little bit on for himself and offer them to Belinda when he next saw her.

In pre-internet days it was much easier to turn up little unseen gems all over the place and I strongly felt my boxwood (absolutely not plastic) seal was one such treasure.

The timing was perfect. The big fair at Olympia (when Olympia was still considered a "big fair") was going to be on and my friend would pop in to see Belinda at her stand during set up, offering her his few gathered odds and ends together with my seal. I'd told him that it had to be £200 as I just couldn't find another (maybe a bit punchy), he then added about £30 for himself. Mum of course was still assured it was plastic and open mouthed at my audacious pricing.

A couple of days later I got the "blow-by-blow" account back from my friend. He'd gone to the fair and seen Belinda setting up. Offering his little parcel of wares alongside my seal to her. As this was going on, the other dealers in the hall were out and about, setting up and trawling for stock. Another leviathan of the trade, the great Polly de Courcy-Ireland, then the leading dealer of Treen in the U.K (if not the World), was passing by the stand as the deal was going down.

Belinda bought the fob seal straight away for the price asked and only moments later, with my friend still loitering, Polly circled by again, then swooped in.

"Belinda, how much for this little seal?"

The price just paid was simply doubled and Polly snapped it up so quickly Belinda couldn't help but remark,

"You'll probably make quite a bit on that Polly"

to which the reply came instantly back,

"Oh no, I'm not going to sell it! In all my years I've never seen a fruitwood seal, it's for my own collection."

You can imagine both my utter delight at being right and absolute horror at considerably underselling it. Still, I was able to recount the tale to Mum several times in the years that followed whenever doubt crept in. How that little Georgian seal had quickly passed from one illustrious hand to another, ending up in what was commonly regarded as a world class collection. Sometimes of course Mum would then remind me of the many more purchases that had not ended so well, had ended in empty pockets, swearing and tears. It preserved a healthy balance, a cynicism which knocked any pretence out of me at just the right moment, though she wisely never condemned out of hand anything else as "just a bit of plastic" ever again.

Chapter 19: Never say never again

There are moments you never forget in this business. One day many years ago looking at the pictures of a "Continental Bowl" in a sale in Canada I found myself taken further back to working away at Sotheby's in deepest, darkest Sussex.

I really didn't appreciate how spoilt I'd been in the years I spent there. Silver was disgorged into my little office from every corner of the globe. The entire Sotheby's multinational machine emptied the contents of palaces, castles, stately homes and bank vaults at my feet, one blue plastic box at a time (after, of course, the London department had picked out all the choicest and most valuable items).

Once or twice a day another blue plastic pannier was dragged in by the porters and I'd usually end up shouting "just stick it over there", whilst pointing to an already massing pile. I didn't know any different and my previous experience at Christie's South Kensington had fitted a similar bill. At the time I assumed this was simply the way every Auction House worked (I can say with authority and hindsight it is absolutely not).

I was also present at the end of the "great sales",

maybe they carried on a couple years more after I left, but no, I was witnessing the throws of the last great hurrah.

Don't get me wrong, wonderful things are still bought and sold every day, but those monumental, centuries old family and state collections which came to auction and were not selectively studded but absolutely rammed packed full of the rarest and finest, their days are gone.

The Roseberry sale came to Sussex but only for a viewing. It was a single glossy hardback catalogue job and museum quality pieces littered every page. The assembled treasures arrived, unconventionally one Friday afternoon in the back of a second hand car driven incognito up to London by the the head porter and his sidekick John who was in his 60's then and sported a wonderful handlebar moustache.

John was almost universally disliked by everyone as he had been portering for so long that he hadn't a kind word for any member of staff. I must confess I liked John, even knowing he held me in no special or particular regard to that of my colleagues, though the fact I was "working class and very common" went some way to ameliorating the worst of his excesses.

I'd sometimes spend a minute or two with John before lunch and would ask for his, often pithy, reminisces of past company worthies.

"What about ....., John, what was he like?"

"He was a ***t "

"and his assistant?"

"He was a ***t too, they're all ***ts every one of them, a bunch of lazy, over privileged ***ts"

We shall never sadly see the likes of John again.

The head porter who accompanied John when they went to fetch the gilded and glowing treasures was a man so densely morose that light bent around him. He grunted at me two or three times over the years but I cannot recall he ever smiled or communicated much more than that, though well paid, his was not a happy lot.

When they arrived the Roseberry treasures were stacked unceremoniously on steel shelves in the store room, sixteenth century cup on sixteenth century cup, quite, quite ridiculously, fabulously, gloriously packed in. I stood watching as the then "Big Boss" dropped in with his secretary in tow. Going on to be a major television "personality", he displayed his ability to communicate and engage a crowd as he picked up and described in detail to his trusty servant and the lingering accrued departmental flotsam, every aspect of the pieces before him.

I was savvy enough to stand there tight lipped as he misdescribed and invented various terms and histories for each and every item. You would think, statistically or even out of dumb luck one of the "facts" he disclosed would be correct but he had a genius to speak utterly believable inexactitudes with such conviction that only anyone who actually knew what they were doing would know. After that, for him, the world of television quickly beckoned.

Amongst the Roseberry treasures was something I'd never come across before (in Antiques you're always learning). It was a superb German sixteenth century Baptismal Font or Bowl, absolutely plastered with a genealogy of engraved family arms, parcel gilt and heavy as lead. I did, privately, take a moment to nurse it in my arms, it was everything a piece of silver should be so I was not surprised at the £100-150,000 estimate or the final price of over £300,000 for it.

It's here, after something of a detour (apologies) I

return to the start of this story. A picture of a "Continental Bowl" in a Canadian Auction estimated for $800-1200.

It was not the same bowl, but I believed it too was a Baptismal Bowl, German and of the same period, though this time a series of extremely fine engraved Biblical scenes surrounded the vessel in rectangular panels, it was larger too.

Excitement abounded, this, if bought for estimate was the sort of thing that could set you up for life. The sale wasn't a live bidding auction, just the catalogue was available online, so I set about asking for more images and then called through to book a phone bid.

When I called through I eventually got to speak to the expert in charge who also happened to be the Vice President of the whole (large) company. I chatted to him briefly to double check it didn't have "Made in Taiwan" stamped on the bottom, no it was all fine. Then I asked if I could have a telephone bid on the lot, this near enough as I can remember, was the conversation which we had:

Auctioneer: "I'm sorry we can't give you a phone bid on the lot."

Me: "Look I know I haven't dealt with you before, but if that's a problem I can provide references from other people and if it helps I used to work for Sotheby's..."

Auctioneer: "No it's not that, I'm sorry but we don't have anyone to take a bid at this point. All our lines are booked, even mobiles. If we could I'd do it but it's simply not possible. I hope you understand?"

Me: "Er, well. I really am very keen on the lot, I'm even happy to start it off at the high estimate of $1200. Are you sure, absolutely sure there's no way I could get a phone bid on the bowl?"

Auctioneer: "Believe me it's just not possible, sorry. But if it helps I can take a commission bid now from you?"

Me: "Hmmm, I'm not...I didn't really want to leave a bid, but if there's no other option"

Auctioneer: "No, there isn't"

Me: "Well, okay then, I'll have to leave a bid"

Auctioneer: "Okay, just let me get a pen. Right it's Lot 112, Continental Bowl estimate $800-1200, yes and just to remind you our buyers premium of 20% plus any applicable taxes will be payable on the hammer amount"

Me: "Yes that's fine"

Auctioneer: "So your bid is?"

Me: "Fifty five thousand dollars"

(Silent Pause)

Auctioneer: "Would you like a phone bid?"

After all that I wouldn't and didn't. I'd already left him more than I could reasonably beg, borrow and steal on the bowl but chances like that don't come along very often. Sadly, on the day it made $85,000 so I wasn't even the underbidder (which believe me, is always a relief). I can imagine what that bowl then went on to sell for and what it might fetch today, but perhaps I'd rather not. Still that exchange with a Canadian Auctioneer has always stayed with me, an Auctioneer who I hope learned never to say "never" again.

Chapter 20: Fame is the Spur(t) part 1 "all the chairs have arms"

Television? That's just something you watch surely? At least it was in my family. A large wooden effect box with a tambour roll top front which would conceal the horror of its purpose when not in use. A small lace Doily would support a cut glass vase of flowers with large photographs flanking either side. The sheer abandon of balancing two full pints of water upon a throbbing, crackling leviathan of electricity was justified by the simple fact no one owned their televisions at the time, they were simply hired from Radio Rentals.

As a boy being sent, back and forth, to change the channels on the black plastic control panel, just to the right of the screen, I was, I thought, as close to the television as I would ever get. How could I have suspected, that just like my namesake in Charlie and the Chocolate factory, I would not merely be glued to it but one day end up inside it, condemned, peering out, wondering what the hell was going on.

Working at Sotheby's the call came from the BBC, not to me in particular, but the venerable institution as a whole. "Would you send us some people to be on a new show?"

I did not jump at the chance, not many did (it was the 90's and the idea of appearing on television, within the antiques trade, was considered far more vulgar and damaging than it is today). However there were two important points about volunteering for the mission that held a great appeal. Firstly it was an extra day off and secondly I learned it was being filmed at the Pebble Mill studios, only a stones throw away (rather than a pebbles) from my family home. The opportunity for a long weekend back home was far too good to miss.

It was a revival of "Going for a Song", not that I knew what that was at the time, but it was a sort of antiques guessing game which had first launched Arthur Negus to fame back in the early 70's. This was to be amongst the first of the daytime TV antiques programmes, long before any producer had even dreamt of that now stalwart rhyming slang for someone you didn't particularly like in the antiques trade (Bargain Hunt).

The important thing here was that the "expert" was paired with a jolly minor celebrity (musicians, newsreaders or comical pianists, all recognisable enough to occupy Countdown's Dictionary Corner). The celebrity was there to provide banter and the "expert" was expected to be reasonably good enough within their discipline to impart some useful information, to make a good fist of it, or more precisely not to know so little as to fuck the whole thing up.

The joy of "Going for a Song", at least I suspect for the BBC, was it was studio based. Quick to film several episodes in a day and added to which not one member of the public was involved. No one looking into the camera, knocking off their microphone by accident or asking any pesky questions that no one knew the answer to. It was TV gold. Also I cannot recall money ever changing hands, or if it did, it was so crippling little that I have done my best to blot out all memory of it. That was the BBC's way, never ever accuse them of playing fast and loose with the licence fee, it simply is not within their nature.

I arrived at Pebble Mill to see a fair old mix of folk awaiting the arrival of the host (a breathless Michael Parkinson in a cricket top and trousers). Besides myself there was a local dealer who sold mainly expensive curtains to well-to-do housewives under the pretence of antiques, an elderly collector from the North East who had clearly also lent the programme makers numerous objects for the show (so HAD to be included) and, much to my surprise a very pretty and outrageously clever girl I knew from college who was a junior specialist herself and who I had really rather liked, though the handsome six foot blond athlete that accompanied her and casually draped himself all over her at any opportunity, shelved any other hopes beyond a TV appearance I may have had that day.

Filming began and we were marched into the studio, in alternating pairs by an assistant, who then ushered me to one side.

"Can I have a word?"

"Yes, yes of course."

"Just over here. I wanted to say that the chairs…"

"Yes?" I nodded

"Well, the chairs all have arms" he gingerly communicated to me.

I looked puzzled, what was I supposed to do with this information that the chairs all had arms? What was my response to this revelation and why was I the only one made privy to it?

My puzzlement must have been clear to the studio assistant, who continued, in a much more quieter, whispering tone:

"We can get you one without arms…if that might be more comfortable for you?"

It clicked. Would I fit in the chairs! The cheeky little bastard. I should say that whilst I am now a "heavyweight" of the antiques world back then I was, although not svelte, never that, a perfectly well turned out, off the peg three piece suited figure and the comment clearly did warrant, though not elicit, some kind of a smack.

Filming began and nerves evaporated as antiques were placed before me and I acquitted myself reasonably well, though stumbled slightly with a painting (never my strong suit) valuing it at cautious fifteen thousand pounds when it's insurance value was three quarters of a million. It was all jolly good fun and at least, unlike many antiques programmes today, it actually featured antiques on and throughout it.

I filmed three more times on the show and thought to have had my full "fifteen minutes", or more importantly four deliciously long weekends at home. But, unbeknownst to me I was just like Daniel Craig's character in the film Layer Cake as Michael Gambon's elderly mob boss turns and assures him "you're not getting out, your just getting in, getting started" and so I was.

The Millennium lay ahead as "Going for a Song" rather unjustifiably perished. The TV of the old was behind us, ahead lay a brand new world of "personalities" of bright orange presenters, of game shows, of "Googling" all the answers, of engaging the wider public and everything that would bring with it.

Chapter 21: Fame is the Spur(t) part two "a face for radio"

It had been a year or eighteen months since I'd left Sotheby's, there really is only so long you can keep living in a caravan park (accommodation problems exacerbated by crippling low pay). Back home and free wheeling, I was, though I didn't know it at the time, blissfully happy. Like most people who have everything they could ever want I found myself a little bored. The danger was that my restless boredom coincided with seeing an advert in the back of the ATG (Antiques Trade Gazette) for "experts" for a new television show. At first I passed it by but then thought how my family had loved seeing me briefly on Going for a Song and that it might be a welcome diversion to the pleasant monotony. The key attraction about applying was that it involved almost no effort whatsoever. Writing a short ten minute letter and sending it off, basically just the price of a First Class stamp (back then 27p). When I strolled around the corner, to the lanes small red George VI letterbox to post it, it was with the same degree of hope, rather than expectation, with which you buy a lottery ticket. Something might come of it but you didn't hold your breath.

Two weeks later, when it was all but forgotten, a call came, could I pop down to Bristol for an interview?

It was the middle of summer, very hot and I didn't really want to drive all the way down the M5 with the holiday makers dragging a hundred wretched caravans behind them in the sweltering heat. When it came to it I didn't want to leave my comfortable surroundings but Mum was insistent, telling me in no uncertain terms that I had to go, so I did as I was told.

The drive was a detour to purgatory. The little green car I drove back then, even with all its windows rolled down (both of them), blustering in a deafening gale which drowned out the car radio, was not enough to prevent it being hotter than an oven. I am let's say a "free perspirer" in these situations. Swathes of kitchen towel had been cunningly deployed to mop up the sweat, just as a can of powerful 70's deodorant (Brut) did it's best to mask and freshen up my struggling suited remains. To say I was not at my best at the end of the drive may have been an understatement.

Once I'd arrived in Bristol and found where I was supposed to go, parking the car was to prove its own Herculean labour. Eventually I found a space but only by placing scruples to one side and blocking, then almost reversing into, some frail grey haired Bristolian motorist who still had the wherewithal to communicate her displeasure at my "on road manoeuvre" with the pithiest of hand gestures. I checked and only had two hours of parking before a £100 fine kicked in and at the time I did not have the £100, so timekeeping became my priority. I set off as briskly as a hot fat man in a suit can, towards the appointed venue. It was an old church which had been converted into a saleroom, all the time nervously checking the remaining hundred and four minutes counting down on my late Great Uncle's long service gold wristwatch, worn only on special occasions.

As I arrived it was made clear that mine had not been a special invitation. Hoards of every description of antiques dealer or valuer littered what had been made into a reception area. Much to my surprise I was seated next to an important Sotheby's Head of Department (won't say which one) languorous and confidently attiring a plastic chair as if it were Chippendale (there's a clue). He was never seen again.

My confidence ebbed away and my pressing thought was now that I only had one hour and thirty five minutes left on the meter and the Wardens were definitely about.

Thankfully my wait didn't last long, people were

being called in and out faster than burgers popping out of a McDonalds drive thru window, though less gracefully. Soon it became my turn and I faced a scruffy collection of BBC Bristol's finest. No niceties were observed and the questions, hastily cobbled together antiques shibboleths from a tattered Miller's Guide, came thick and fast:

"Can you name three Majolica factories for us?"

"Wedgwood, Minton and George Jones"

"Ok and some Art Deco potters?"

"Susie Cooper, Clarice Cliff…"

"Any others?"

"…Carter, Stable & Adams, er I mean Poole pottery"

"Fine."

There were a few others blasted at me as I answered quickly back. The dour and slightly terse inquisitor ticked a form appropriately to my responses, good or bad I didn't know. Then I was asked for a brief, very brief camera test. Attempting to engage my stone faced monosyllabic foe, hoping to break the very thick ice, I joked "Well my Mum says I've more a face for radio"

"Yes" came back the immediate and steely reply. That it seemed was that, out the door and "Next!" Happily I got back to the car just in time and sped off home, clutching the now red hot Sun drenched steering wheel with discarded sweat laden kitchen towel to stop my fingers burning. I didn't even get the offer of my petrol money (God bless the BBC).

Much to my amazement, given quite how earnestly churlish my inquisitor had been, I was asked along to screen test proper at one of the first filming days of a new programme called "Flog It", though this time it was to be in Birmingham which wasn't going to be a problem.

I turned up to find an old college acquaintance was screen testing too. All we had to do was sit down and value something for a member of the public then bugger off. Rummaging through the queue I found a very nice Chinese bronze figure, not worth much then but I could talk about it and the owner was a genteel lady who seemed easy enough to talk to. With the cameras poised and a mic fitted it all got a bit tense, the owner was clearly a little nervous, so I thought to break the ice with the only antiques joke I could remember and the oldest one at that:

"You know what an expert really is don't you?"

"Er, no" she nervously replied

"Well X is an unknown quantity and spurt is a drip under pressure"

She laughed and then relaxed. We filmed a short two minute piece and what I said about the bronze may or may not have been utter rubbish, but it seemed to do the trick.

Only now, some twenty years later, do I realise that I could have said that day it was made of Swiss cheese on the Moon by Clangers and the producers wouldn't have batted an eye lid. Unfortunately academic rigour has never really been a key requirement for "Antiques TV" or valued by the majority of those who make it, only an easy manner and the ability to tell a good joke or at least a bad joke well.

Chapter 22: Swap Shop

Dealers and collectors buy and sell things to one another and always (speaking purely as a dealer) hopefully money, a large amount of money, is involved. There is of course an exception, another altogether different type of deal, which can be struck. A deal where no money changes hands, usually agreed between colleagues of the trade, that of the "swap".

I'm not solely blaming Noel Edmonds or the hours spent as a young boy watching Saturday morning's "Multi-coloured Swap Shop" (BBC 1976-82) and having my mind warped that "fair exchange is no robbery" and swapping can be fun. Though my experience since has proved that to be anything but the case.

Early forays into swapping had seen me lose an Irish silver cream jug and Victorian mustard pot to a twenty-four carat bastard of a jeweller and a rather gaudy sovereign ring which Dad gave me in exchange for a beautiful yet almost worthless Victorian silver pocket watch and chain. Experience, you must understand, had not just burnt my fingers, it had grabbed both hands and pressed them palm down onto the hot stove until they blistered. Though both stubborn and wilful, who was I to learn my lesson?

Years, decades had passed and it had been a long time since I had swapped anything. Maybe an odd or end had gone, like the cased fruit knife and fork exchanged with Portobello dealer "donut" for a Georgian unmarked filigree box, but that was all quite equitable. Maybe that had lulled me into a false sense of security, but there were bigger, much bigger, deals which lay ahead.

The week in question, when the whole affair began, started off well and better than most as "The Journal" had arrived that morning.

One of the first things I was instructed to do as an Auctioneer (by my venerable employers) was to join the Silver Society. I was more than happy to do it as they, not I, were paying the dues, though sadly I never quite had the time to make it to meetings, almost always held in central London (fine IF you live there)! However I did relish the publication of the annual Journal, which could arrive at almost any time during the year (publication was sporadic) but which meant it always came as the most marvellous and welcome surprise.

The Silver Society Journal was a collection of academic papers on almost every aspect of silver. Whilst some articles would be too high brow for the likes of me "the role and influence of Viennese

Operatic set designs in the manufacture of the Princess Strelnitz gilt toilet service" (sorry I've completely made that up just so you get the gist) others would be more practical. The survey of a Goldsmiths life and who he worked with, or the marks of a particular region or family reappraised and identified. It was always a fascinating read and served, possibly rashly, to fan the flames of my enthusiasm for antique silver to a white heat. It was always a financially precarious time when my antiques blood was fully up.

Most of the public imagine that in the world of antiques we do deals in the most comfortable and luxurious of settings. A decade or more of "Lovejoy" on the Telly conjures up scenes of discussing deals in the snug of a country hotel, sipping brandy from a lead crystal balloon, next to a roaring fire with a stunning blonde, or explaining the finer points of a renaissance sculpture in the marble lined halls of an Italian Palazzo to a gaunt, immaculately bearded Count sporting a gold rimmed monocle. The truth is, that after reading my copy of The Journal, I was meeting up with a dealer the very next day in a mutually equidistant Sainsbury's Car Park, next to a saleroom we both knew. But why? Well despite a lifetime of bitter experience to the contrary we were meeting up to do a swap.

I was hoping to do deal for a tankard which I'd first seen over a year earlier. It was unascribed, bearing only an unidentified and repeated makers mark with no other clue as to where it was from. Despite its anonymity the price was certainly not insubstantial (never that), indeed it was much more than I could possibly afford when I had called the dealer in question, but of course I had a plan.

I knew this piece had been kicking around the trade for a bit. Purchased, let's be kind and say "by committee" on the East Coast of England more than a year earlier, it had been offered, then shunned by the great and the good of the London silver trade. He didn't want it, nor him, nor him, they all shook their heads, covered their eyes and then ears like a line of brass, or maybe silver, monkeys. It was a mystery item that almost nobody wanted to own.

Happily the tankard escaped a metropolitan fate, fleeing to the provinces and to a dealer I liked very much in that he was always game, always prepared to take a "punt" and back his own judgement. When everyone else was screaming and running in the opposite direction he would raise his hand to bid. Besides this bravery he also knew what he didn't know and that, in the antiques business at least, is a rare quality and placed him high on my list of regard and even better than that he always loved to do a deal.

In the months prior to this I had, (purely out of good fortune or dumb luck), acquired two very fine Georgian silver tea caddies. One privately from the family for whom it was made, another by fluke and happenstance from a French EBay seller. The first, after disposing of the rest of the collection I acquired owed me nothing, the second cost only a few hundred pounds yet they were, at the time, happily selling for three or four thousand pounds a piece in London and selling like hot cakes. Here then was a tasty dish to set before the King, or at least offer as a straight swap.

When no money changes hands both parties need to be certain that they are doing better out of the deal, maybe it's just human nature but it's certainly an antiques dealer's one.

In this case I was proposing to exchange two previously unseen (therefore very desirable) shit-hot silver tea caddies for a tankard, which although it dated back to the seventeenth century and was in good order, was only marked with a single anonymous makers punch. A tankard which had been knocked back by every other silver dealer in the country and had not garnered a single bit of private interest in over a year online and display at several antiques fairs. Understandably, when I suggested the swap he absolutely bit my hand off.

The small market town where we had agreed to meet stood halfway between where we both lived. I set off on a glorious sunny morning with Mum sat beside me in the passenger seat of the car clutching the two stunningly beautiful silver tea caddies in her hands wearing a look of both worry and disapproval over the impending prospect of her fickle offspring soon giving both of them away.

About noon we pulled into the Sainsbury's car park to see the elder statesman of the trade waiting in the sunshine beside his much, much bigger car. Having exchanged our hellos Mum passed me out the two caddies which I then offered up.

Smiling and buoyant he looked at each one in turn and was clearly absolutely delighted (though tried his best not to show it) at the prospect, in only a few short minutes time, of swapping a pig's ear, for not one but two silk purses.

In the meantime I inspected the tankard as I had only previously seen it online. I took my time and checked the feel and weight and most importantly of all I carefully checked the maker's mark under my 10x achromatic jewellers loupe. It was struck deeply and clearly four times on the side of the body and four times on the cover. The elaborate cast twin dolphin thumb-piece did have a little old solder repair to it but besides that it was a glorious thing. Forgetting all the other swaps I'd done before in my life which had gone horrifically wrong I took the plunge.

"Alright then?" I said. He eagerly nodded back and then without further ado, we exchanged goods. He put the caddies into the boot of his car swifter than the speed of light and locked it shut. That clearly was a deal not to be undone and, now very broadly smiling, he handed me the tankard.

He was aware (as many dealers were) that I spent most of my time squirreling away at books and ledgers looking for obscure attributions to odd marks that most people had given up on.

"So what's this going to be Michael, American Colonial?"

he chuckled, not maliciously just in fun as he knew, as I did, that he (and every other dealer who had seen it in the last year and a half) had already checked EVERY reference book on Earth to identify the mark without success.

He knew he had gotten the better of me, he knew it from every single page he'd turned in every single book he'd scoured and every other dealer and collector he had shown it to without success. Had I stumbled yet again, though now terribly so? Losing two of the loveliest Georgian tea caddies you'll ever see simply on a whim, on a foolish rush of blood? My Mum looked despairingly on. But did I mention that the day before, just before, I had received my Silver Society Journal? Yes I must have mentioned it, I did love the Journal and always made a point of reading it, cover to cover, as soon as it arrived.

The first article that I had read only the day before, barely minutes before making the deal I was now concluding in the full glamour of a Sainsbury's Car Park had been on the first seventeenth century silversmiths working in Worcester.

Two brothers, born in Worcester, but who had been apprenticed and worked for a while in London, having then decided to return back home and become Worcester's only Goldsmiths. Whilst a few pieces of silver were known in private collections by the elder (John) only a handful of church plate had been seen by the younger (Samuel). Nothing else, the article's authors had stressed, was known. Not even a worn and bent old spoon could be found after years of looking, no nothing, except as I'd remembered whilst first reading the article a very fine tankard proudly displayed on another dealer's website as "unascribed"

He was still looking at me smiling broadly as I paused for a second before deciding to honestly answer his question.

"No it's not American, it's Worcester"

I simply, cleanly and perhaps a little brutally, replied.

"Eh?" the broad smile he bore was still firmly fixed, he was after all a true professional. His happy demeanour was preserved after the bomb had gone off, except perhaps around the eyes. Those windows to the soul, only a moment earlier both bright and sparkling, had paled and deadened and I believe in that moment he could have thrown both caddies into a ravine had one been nearby. Realisation had broken that I stood before him holding a (or more correctly "the") Worcester silver tankard.

I would like to tell you something like that happens once a week, or month or even year but the truth is that much of antiques dealing is a string of bitter disappointments, always losing out to someone with a million in their pocket to each and every hundred in yours (even if they often don't know what they're doing). But now and again fate, God or luck levels off the playing field, maybe even slopes it off in your direction. So at last, long last my swap-shop curse was broken.

Chapter 23: Beware of A.Dick

I never returned to full time auction employment after leaving Sotheby's (I mean honestly, where do you go after that?) Besides, as Darth Vadar would have said "my journey to the dark side (dealing with a bit of TV thrown in for good measure) was complete". Though that didn't mean I wasn't still regularly asked to work for any number of salerooms.

Unfortunately the thought of sitting in a small dark room, hunched over for five days a week tapping away at a computer, no longer held much appeal. Truthfully very few auctioneers were the size of Sotheby's and really required or merited the services of a full time silver specialist. Bearing that in mind, and only when needs pressured musts to an intolerable level, I could sometimes be persuaded to "consult".

Being an auction house consultant is far more glamorous than it sounds. It really just means they pay you a little bit for a few days work rather than a lot for the whole year.

I undertook the duties for friends who were auctioneers, though I did fall into doing it, for a number of years, for one large North Country saleroom.

They were a friendly family firm and everything was very relaxed. In truth if I could ever have slipped back into the auction world full time it would have been here, save for one thing, the enormous distance from home.

The first few times I drove the 170 miles there I would stay over at a B&B and do the return leg the day after, but I never slept. There is a level of "uncomfortable" it is difficult to imagine unless you've stayed in an attentive, well meaning, country "guest house hotel". No it was not for me. This was easily solved though as I was much younger, much fitter and much happier to get up early and work like the Devil.

From then on I set off at around 5.00am to arrive around 7.30am (ish) and work until every lot had been catalogued or valued (around 3.30pm if I was lucky). Then I'd drive back to collapse at home like a race horse that had just run the National twice, recovering by doing almost nothing the next day.

When I went up I didn't even break for lunch, but to their credit I would be constantly offered tea by passing members of various departments as the door to my office was kept open. At lunch time one or two flapjacks made by the in-house restaurant would be brought up on a disposable paper plate. I did ask a few times for the recipe but the catering staff remained tight lipped. The flapjacks were as buttery as you could imagine but also surprisingly crisp, crisp in a good way. If I've wondered about anything over the years, if one thing has haunted me, then it was how the hell they made those flapjacks so utterly delicious. I've tried all sorts of recipes and methods but to no avail. I wouldn't be surprised to find out they used cocaine instead of baking powder, they were that addictive. I came for the cataloguing, but I stayed for the flapjacks (oh, and the money).

My tenure as "consultant" went from strength to strength in as much as more and more AND MORE silver would come in for sale with every subsequent visit. At first the office, which had deep floor to ceiling shelves on three full walls would be laden with objects. Then it began to spill onto the desk, the chair beside mine, then the floor. Pieces were stacked high and low and then everywhere.

I could still catalogue everything in a day. Though as time went on I particularly began to despise cataloguing canteens. Canteens aren't hard to catalogue, in fact they're easy, but you must, MUST check the hallmarks on every single piece. Just because it may all arrive in a nice fitted period case and there's twelve of everything, doesn't mean some larcenous guest at a dinner party in 1923 didn't abscond with a butter knife or a soup spoon for which the owner then had to order a replacement. One date letter awry, one different maker not noted and all hell would break loose. No I did not like cataloguing canteens, well I did not like the time it took.

As my time became more valued and pressured one of the senior general full time cataloguers said he'd be happy to pick up any odds and ends I couldn't manage in the one precious day that I had. Usually everything was fine but I did, I confess, leave the odd canteen or boring Georgian tea set for him to do. Besides they were all very straight forward lots which wouldn't cause any problems.

One catalogue deadline day I was called up to attempt a rather ominous pile. Not one but two full family collections of silver added to all the usual suspects. Every shelf, every spare bit of space, even the usually unused shelf tops (slightly out of reach) had silver on them. It was going to be a weeks work in a day and I was going to do it.

I didn't stop for tea or even for flapjacks, I ploughed on. Occasionally other members of staff would pop in for a friendly natter but I cut them short as politely as I could. By noon the majority of the shelves were done, a hundred lots or so, leaving only the desk, floor and hard to reach places, I dug in for a long afternoon.

About three-ish I was fading a bit, having driven and worked non stop for almost eleven hours and then the senior cataloguer, who helped me out, chose this moment to pop his head around the door.

"How's it going?"

"Fine, fine" I replied still scribbling away at a pad (I hand wrote all my valuations) "Just these and that and those to do" I pointed around the room.

"Well it's getting on, if you want me to do the…"

"Canteen?" I interrupted

He half smiled and shrugged, "Yes, alright then I'll do the canteen, but don't forget the stuff on the very top shelf."

I looked up to see a Victorian dressing box and a casually stacked Georgian three piece tea set, cheap sheet silver as many of them are and dead boring.

By four (as late as I ever stayed on these round trip days), excluding the canteen, I still had the shelf with the dressing box and tea set to do. Looking up at it I thought my colleague could easily do those as well and I left a note that he should quickly polish them off when he did the canteen. Hurtling downstairs I stopped only for seconds at the canteen to stuff a couple of napkined flapjacks in my suit pockets for the journey home. Twelve hours, just about on today's minimum wage and with a 170 mile return trip home still to do, I set off with only a few mouthfuls of golden buttery crispness to sustain me. I feel tired now just thinking about it.

A few weeks passed and duly I was sent out a copy of the "Fine Sale" catalogue to admire my handiwork of several weeks past. It all looked, as it usually did, glossily good. That was until I saw both the illustration and cataloguing of a very boring Georgian three piece tea set I had abandoned to my colleague on that very top shelf without even looking. I got up and ran to the phone.

All, well most, silver is hallmarked (I won't go into detail it would take a year to discuss the matter properly) but around the end of the eighteenth century and with growing industrialisation and trade, many corners of the globe, especially those coloured pink, had grown familiar enough with our own British hallmarks to see them as a guarantee of quality of silver and workmanship.

If you were a working silversmith and had travelled halfway across the globe to set up in some colonial enclave you would often fashion (or have made for you) a series of punches which would imitate those British hallmarks people were familiar with, to be struck alongside your own maker's punch. They're known today as "pseudo" or "colonial" hallmarks and can be found on a variety of pieces from Canada, to the Cape, from to Canton or India, but they can also be found upon rare early silver made in Australia.

One of the most prominent and sought after (really, really sought after) Australian silversmiths is A.Dick. I'm not being pejorative, his name was Alexander Dick, sometimes stamping his initials "AD" alongside pseudo marks or actually stamping his surname in full "A.DICK". It was those marks that I could see illustrated on a boring Georgian tea set estimated at what was now a crushingly modest £7-900.

I called the saleroom straight away and as the phone rang, honestly my first instinct was to ask to book a phone bid on the tea set, but sadly scruples intruded and as reception answered to put me through to the "main man" my course was clear.

"You've got to change the estimate and description on that tea set right away" I urgently announced.

"It's only a three piece Michael…"

"No. It's Australian, we really have to change the estimate!"

"Alright, how much?"

I paused for a second. I knew what the very similar Australian three piece tea set had made at Christie's a couple of years earlier, but I did also think "Well, that was Christie's" so I pitched it a little lower.

"£20-30,000. Reserve £20,000...Fixed!!"

There was some umming and ahhing at the other end of the line. Possibly through disbelief (it was a VERY ugly three piece tea set, that must be said) and the majority feeling was to leave it as is and let it make what it makes, but I was named as the cataloguer and adamant that the estimate and description had to change and reflect that we actually knew what we were doing.

That bloody top shelf. If only I'd looked a little closer on the day but then I'd fallen, albeit quite tired and underpaid, into a dreadful trap which awaits all and any in the antiques trade.

I'd taken a quick look, just glanced up without really looking and thought "nothing special" without taking just a few minutes more to confirm it. Familiarity, in this case, with ugly late Georgian tea sets, had bred contempt.

Nine hundred and ninety nine times out of a thousand you will be right, you'll possibly even rebuke yourself for pausing to look. But the time you're wrong, the time you've missed it (and it will come), means you have to remind yourself to look and look carefully, every single time.

Thankfully on the day of the auction it went well. We'd saved the situation early enough with the correct description and estimate for all and every interested party to see it. Bids poured in from around the globe and the £33,000 made by the three piece Christie's set a few years earlier was left standing as ours made £42,000 (plus the slap).

Still it was a fact never lost on me that the one lot that almost slipped through my cataloguing fingers had "A.DICK" stamped on it, had "A.DICK" stamped on it since the day it was made. Now don't tell me that the antiques Gods don't have a sense of humour.

Chapter 24: One, two, buckle my shoe

Are things in antiques ever meant to be? Do we set off randomly each day, lurching from purchase to purchase, from sale to sale, or are just rewards (or comeuppances) simply waiting for the time they know we're destined to find them? I don't ask the question frivolously but with some solid cause, though it all begins a long time ago, with a very wise old man wearing a piece of cardboard about his neck.

"Watch out" Mum said, as we were manning the stand at yet another busy Sunday antiques fair in the heart of London, back through the mists of time. A slightly eccentric figure was directly approaching the stand, heading towards us and our cabinets with intent. He was almost Professorial in looks, were it not for the large, homemade placard he was wearing, fashioned from string and cardboard, hanging about his neck, which no one could fail to miss (well, that of course was the point). It bore the legend, emphatically and boldly applied in dark black marker pen "I BUY BUCKLES". That was to be the first ever time I was to meet my buckle guru.

Years and friendship followed and I, always reluctant in the extreme to socialise with anyone, was gently coaxed to visit him and his wife for the odd day.

Lunch would be provided and we would talk all things silver and indeed all things buckle. My interest in the very niche field of silver buckles had always been centred around any odd provincial makers or marks, but my buckle guru's knowledge and researches went far, far deeper than that.

Visit after visit (I was happy to return and more surprisingly they were happy to let me) I just listened, listened and listened. Sensibly keeping my mouth shut. At first it was curiosity and politeness to charming hosts, but as with all things, if you listen to a real expert on their subject, talking passionately and informatively about it, for long enough, you get suckered in. By my third visit it was too late to turn back and I think the buckle-bug had bitten me, though I didn't know it at the time.

I'd already learnt in that short while, to look at different styles and periods of buckles, to appreciate the work of particular makers and to realise that nothing, well almost nothing had been written on the subject.

One small tome existed, written many years ago by a now famous television "Art Detective" whilst he was still at school. That I was told was "a good attempt" but also that "over fifty percent of it was nonsense". Beyond that only a brief, but reliable, paperback guide from Northamptonshire Museum Services existed (due to the towns famous association with Shoe making and their local Museum collection). My buckle guru had bought the last few of copies when they were remaindered for 50p each and then let me have one for a tenner! His genteel demeanour fooled many but he was sharper than a razor. Still no good book can ever cost too much, and this was still a bargain at ten pounds.

I gradually came to realise the general lack of interest in and rather stagnant market of, silver buckles, was in no small part due to the efforts of my mentor. When he did find a competitor collector (a rare beast indeed) he would befriend them, advise them and ultimately "nobble them" (his own words). I hadn't been any kind of a threat in that vein, though I was always able to help in identifying odd marks which weren't his main area of study. When I eventually confessed an interest in buying the odd buckle myself, I thought it would have been in very poor taste to go up against him after all the knowledge he had shared with me. So after tentative negotiations I arrived at a niche little area of buckles to satisfy my interest and wants which in no way conflicted with his. But we also agreed that if any provincial buckles turned up I would probably still at least try to buy them and that it would be the case of "let the best man win" and we were both fine with that, a mutually agreed "nobbling" of one another.

It was probably only a year or two later that I saw a pair of fine large Georgian silver shoe buckles catalogued as "Birmingham, indistinct marks" in an auction in Yorkshire. I knew the saleroom well and had visited many times. An old converted cinema, with a cafe next door that served enormous sausage, bacon and egg cobs for just a couple of pounds. I thought they might be something interesting, not Birmingham at all, though I was also attracted to them by their size and the thought of the sausage, bacon and egg cob I would enjoy if I had to go up and collect them.

Buckles, pairs of shoe buckles, were made in all sizes, though some were ridiculously large (often called "Artois" buckles, named after Louis XVI's brother, the Comte D'Artois who sported frankly enormous buckles in the British Court whilst serving as Ambassador). My buckle guru explained more than once, in a disheartened tone, that these giant buckles, because of their bullion weight, rarely survived. They were Courtly objects of fashion and fashions quickly changed. Imagine going to Court to be seen in last Season's buckles, would there be a greater crime? So, often, these whoppers were exchanged with

Goldsmiths, the value of the silver put against the price of something newer, better and of the very latest style.

This was why spotting a large marked, possibly "not Birmingham" pair in the wild was an event simply too tempting to resist. Unspoken, both I and my mentor bid for the large buckle beasts, neither daring to confess to the other that they had spotted them. I later found out he hadn't been quite sure of what the marks on the buckles were (apart from being certain that they weren't Birmingham), which is probably why I ended up the victor.

On my next visit I did the decent thing and took them with me to show him, to add to his database and put another small brick into the "knowledge wall". I disclosed that whilst they did bear anchor marks (the Birmingham town mark and understandable cause of the auctioneer's confusion) they were in fact Scottish and Scottish Provincial at that.

In the intervening years I'd seen a lot of buckles, more buckles I suspect than almost anybody else on Earth, except for the buckle-master himself. There were, I can tell you now, desperately few Scottish ones. A few pairs from Edinburgh or Glasgow would turn up, very occasionally. Beyond that Scottish

Provincial pairs were insanely rare. If any could be described as "common" (none were) then the title might go to Aberdeen, largely thanks to the efforts of John Leslie and second place maybe to Dundee, maybe. The pair, the large pair I had bought were within the territory of a hen's tooth, William Hannay of Paisley, an anchor also being a Paisley town mark. They were admired and I was congratulated on the find. Only one other Paisley pair were on his database and he had looked in almost every private and institutional collection around the globe. I had found an honest to goodness gem and years of buckle knowledge having been generously poured in through my eyes and ears was finally bearing fruit. Was this then my reward, my "destined" find from the antiques Gods? No, perhaps just a bit of luck and the benefit of really looking.

It was a good eight years later that the story found its end. The visits continued, the looking continued, the joy of Antiques continued, until the day I again saw a description of "possibly Birmingham" appended to a pair of buckles, though this time they were very small.

A listing had appeared on EBay for a pair, not of shoe, but of knee (or breeches) buckles. They fastened up the bottom of your short breeches and were much less valuable than shoe buckles of the same period, but here again there had been some confusion over the marks?

It had been the policy that I would get my hands chopped off if I went to bid for any buckles on EBay and I was happy to leave my buckle guru to it, though this time I realised these were probably, possibly, Paisley, despite the bad pictures on the listing, so it wouldn't strictly be breaking our accord of many years. At least that's what I told myself.

I left, let's say "a few hundred pounds" and was ecstatic to pay only £85 when the listing finally ended. I was quickly congratulated by an email from my mentor who admitted to being the underbidder and (I could tell) was a tiny bit peeved. He had only left so little as he didn't think anyone else would see them and I felt slightly bad but explained, if it helped ease the pain, that I had left quite a bit more than that as I thought they were provincial. It helped a bit I think, but, understandably as with all collectors, not that much.

A few days past and then Postie knocked the door with a small registered envelope to deliver, the tiny pair of knee buckles. EBay's only good point can be that it makes every day feel like Christmas, well every day you get a parcel. I quickly and nervously unwrapped the package. The images had been okay (ish) but not great and a lot can go wrong with a buckle. Odd chapes (the mechanism inside the frame, often steel), breaks or repairs to the silver frame, wear to the marks or decoration, but no, these were little gems. Dirty, unpolished but perfect with nice marks and the original owners initials to the frame. I hadn't looked at the larger pair of Paisley shoe buckles I'd bought almost a decade earlier for some time. It would be nice, I thought, to compare them and then take both the shoe and knee buckles over on my next visit, so I went to dig them out.

Sitting, quietly, having pulled out the baize lined mahogany drawer of the bottom half of a once great, now distressed secretaire desk that laughably functioned as my entire "office" I compared both sets of buckles. I was astonished, I was dumbstruck.

The pair of knee buckles that had just arrived were naïvely engraved with the original owner's initials "WF". As I picked up the shoe buckles and turned them over I saw, though I had forgotten, the very same initials, "WF" engraved by the very same hand.

Paisley buckles are stupidly, impossibly rare. Yet here were the shoe and knee buckles from the very same set, made the better part of 240 years ago, for one man, now reunited, though bought nearly a decade apart and from different ends of the country. Really, what ARE the chances? A million to one sounds hackneyed but about right. It may be that the auction Gods do sometimes play their part. We might just be haphazardly buying the very next bit of old tat that pops up, or we might be just walking down a path towards a handful of wonderful things that we were always supposed to be the custodians of, at least for a time. A little reward for learning, for knowing, and for caring about the small old things that largely get forgotten and left behind.

In memory of my much missed buckle mentor and very good friend, Mr T.

Chapter 25: Treasure Chest

There are some some salerooms that require viewing, some that demand it. Occasionally an auction house is located in a particularly good area and inclined to gather in all sorts of treasures from well-to-do migratory retirees, picking and plucking off their brightest feathers before they fall completely off the perch. Then there are others where "guile" is noticeably absent, and despite the best efforts of successive successful purchasers to stifle reports, news escapes of "wonderful things" abandoned in the bottom of cardboard boxes. Objects which are uncatalogued, unphotographed and unknown. To these sales you beat a hasty path and linger during viewing. Any ten pound box could conceal a hidden gem, or even be one.

This particular saleroom was already famous, well, infamous. The overlooked ancient gold medallion the size of baby's fist bought for the same price as a similar one made out of chocolate at Christmas time. The huge Irish Provincial silver two handled tray bought below scrap because it was catalogued as "20th century American" the proceeds of which kept many dealers going for a month. Then of course there was "the vase". The Chinese vase which, initially estimated at a healthy four to six thousand pounds realised a little under two hundred thousand! What a fabulous result that was, well fabulous at least for the small group of like minded dealers who bought it and then sold it much more quietly a few months later, on the other side of the world, for a smidge under four, four million that is. Yes this was a sale I was (at the time) always eager to view.

I waddled in early, whilst it was quiet and sat myself down before a bank of glass cabinets containing an array of silver, all held in plastic bags and cardboard boxes. Each lot was quietly tipped out onto the counter top and I sifted through it in an intense deafening silence. The porter glared intently on, occasionally trying to engage me in casual conversation, it was as uncomfortable as any visit to the Barbers you could wish to mention. Still, might there be a hidden treasure amongst the tat? No, not this time but I was happier in my mind knowing I hadn't missed a thing and this was why I always had to check.

Had it been any other sale I would have darted straight off after viewing the silver but this was an auction where anything could happen. I strolled around for half an hour, diving under tables, rummaging through all the odd boxes, though to no particular avail. Not one life changing, jewel encrusted golden treasure lay unforgotten beneath a chipped mug or a care worn teddy bear to reward my diligence. It was only as I was leaving, struggling, fighting my way through a blockade of determined almost immovable chatty pensioners, simply there for a "day out" from whichever institution usually confined them, that I happened to walk past the rostrum.

It always had some of the lower value lots from each sale strewn before it, set dressing for the auction day where an ear cringing performance would assault anyone in the room brave enough to sit through the entire proceedings. Auctioneers all have have different styles, different cadences and demeanours picked up instinctively from the people they first worked under and who taught them the way of the gavel. This particular auctioneers mentor had passed away some years earlier, I do not know the cause exactly but it would not surprise me to learn that he may have bored himself to death. He had, after all, done it to many of his bidders over the years. He was long gone, though his appalling auction mannerisms were still very much alive and kicking, kicking everyone who sat through every sale, firmly, up the arse.

Lain on the tables before the rostrum were a repetitive group of ten or so Victorian workboxes, laid out in a wooden row, like bricks, like a barricade. They were common currency at the time. Every antiques shop, fair and centre would have one or several. Often confused for Tunbridge ware they were in fact the very nemesis of our superior British souvenirs, German bandwork boxes. Early in the nineteenth century "Tunbridge ware" makers had developed a system of producing intricate topographical scenes from wood mosaics made of rods of stained timbers, all glued together and then sliced. The apparatus for this process now housed in the Birmingham Museum and Art Gallery as part of the Pinto Collection, Edward Pinto being the great authority and collector who authored the seminal book on all things "Treen".

These however were German bandwork boxes, cruder, quicker and much cheaper to produce, though it must be said, still very decorative. They started flooding into the British market around the 1860's and it wasn't long before the sales of Tunbridge ware began to falter from the competition. Sadly so often "cheaper" will defeat "better" in a straight fight for the public's pocket throughout the ages. The sheer fecundity of supply meant they were now, as antiques, commanding very little money. I had bought a hingeless walnut example, gutted of its interior for a mere tenner as a boy to store my then burgeoning selection of antique oddments in. The selection on view were clearly someone's entire life's collection and looking in the catalogue each description was lazily identical, "Victorian walnut work box" with a matching "£40-60" estimate, yet looking along the line one of the boxes, about the seventh or eighth along stood starkly out, despite it's identical catalogue description to all the others. At first I thought it might be mis-lotted but then I remembered where I was, this was the land where the one eyed man was king, even if he was blinking and wearing an eye patch on the wrong side.

I should say now that like most antiques dealers I have a thing for boxes, we all do. Don't ask me why but there is something deeply wonderful about a good antique box, be it silver, wood, lacquer or any other material you can think of. For ages I had yearned for a particular type, a coffre fort (strong box) with decorative gilt brass mounts on an oyster veneered base. This was not that but neither was it a ubiquitous Victorian German band work box.

Years earlier, at Sotheby's, we had a small silver 17th century box come in for sale. It was of a style predominantly made by Huguenot refugees that came over after the revocation of the Edict of Nantes in 1685. Silversmiths not free of any of the London companies would make an immediate living by producing small novelties heavily engraved with scrolls, birds cherubs and little mottoes in French or Latin. The most frequently found examples were small oval boxes with a squeeze action catch. Rarer were rectangular or octagonal examples, decorated in the same manner but often with larger scenes of towns or villages. The rarest though were the ones raised on four little ball feet imitating the travelling trunks and boxes of the period with gently domed covers and central swing handles. I had seen two or three of these miniature silver examples but never the larger wooden boxes which they were based upon, that was of course until I had viewed the "Victorian walnut work box" in this particular sale.

I was careful not to pick it up, or make a fuss, though I did surreptitiously sidle up beside it and quickly feel over the surface for lost veneer or errant repairs. It all seemed fine. I left as nonchalantly as possible and determined if not to buy the box to at least give it my best shot.

The day of the auction arrived and I had registered to bid online. You would only attend this sale in person if forced to, at gunpoint, as the slow, theatrical style of auctioneering could quickly sap any joy and life out of the most optimistic and light hearted of bidders. That it was held on the ground floor was simply a matter of personal safety. Any higher up and at least a couple of people in the room would have found a window to try and jump out of. As usual the sale was painfully slow, but eventually after all the unspectacular silver I'd carefully viewed had not been sold, we arrived at the run of Victorian (and "not Victorian") walnut boxes.

True to estimate the first struggled to make its forty pound start, as did the second, then the third. The hope, the slender hope, was growing as I hovered over the keyboard that all the boxes, including the much rarer one I'd set my heart upon, would do the same. As it came up a forty pound bid came in much more quickly than the previous bids, then fifty, then sixty, then more. Without any of the usual dramatic encouragements of the auctioneer it was running away, quickly into hundreds. I feared the game was up. My chance to finally join in the bidding frenzy came only when three hundred had been reached but that soon doubled to nearly six. Then as suddenly as it had all began the bidders in the room melted away and the hammer fell. There's a breed of local dealer that will always take a punt on something unfamiliar but only ever up to a certain point, usually a round figure, five hundred or a thousand, a "just in case" bid but beyond that they begin to waiver, as they did on this occasion, thank goodness.

It was still early in the day, mid afternoon and I simply couldn't contain my excitement at buying the box. As soon as the lot had been knocked down to me I leapt (this was a time when I could still leap) into the car and sped off to pick it up. Unbeknownst to me the auctioneer had got the "TV people" in that day, filming a stalwart daytime antiques programme, most famous now as rhyming slang in the trade for someone you didn't particularly care for. It was a truly Jacobite event in the sense that it comprised both the "old and young pretender", pretending to know what they were doing. This unfortunately led to me being accosted by a chatty dealer as I was leaving, heading into the car park, a little awkwardly with the box wedged lovingly between my arms and steadied beneath my bearded chin.

"You filming here today are you?"

"No, not me. I don't do this programme, I do…"

"Oh yes, you do Flog It don't you?"

"Yes, that's the one. Once in a blue moon, blink and you'll miss it…if you're lucky" I smiled trying to flee my determined inquisitor, slowly heading further towards the car, but she pursued.

"What we're you doing then? Bidding? Buying?"

I resisted the temptation to motion down with my eyes towards the box I was clearly carrying and reply "yes what do you think this thing is, a lesion?" Instead simply saying with a forced smile:

"Just buying a Victorian box"

She now acknowledged it and taking a moments look replied,

"That IS nice, did it cost much?"

"A bit, a little bit over the estimate. But it's a good thing. Little bit earlier than they said it was in the catalogue" the car was now only a few feet away and freedom beckoned.

"Oh, we'll that doesn't seem quite fair, not if it's older and worth more than they said"

By now the box was on the bonnet and my car keys were feverishly lunging and scratching at the handle to open the doors. I was seconds away from freedom. All at once I got in behind the wheel and swiftly had the box on the seat beside me, I put it's seatbelt on before mine and with my dogged interviewer still now peering and leaning into the passenger side window, I started up the car to deliver my parting shot:

"Well you can always stand a chance of buying a bargain at an auction…

(She nodded and smiled thinking I'd finished my drop of wisdom)

…if the auctioneer doesn't have a fucking clue what they're doing!"

I waved a cheery goodbye just as I said it and her dumbfounded, open mouthed expression of shock and surprise finished the day off nicely.

Upon my return home the box was cleaned (lightly) and waxed, much to the immediate admiration of all that saw it. It had exotic burr veneers and interlacing scrolls all beneath the original brass swing handle to the domed cover which I decided should not be polished. The lock was original as was the escutcheon which happily still held the original steel key!

I've seen one or two since, for sale on the Continent (without keys), at very healthy prices. There was a lovely English oyster veneered version too which came up and sparked a bidding war in a Somerset saleroom some years later. That day I walked away the underbidder at a few thousand not hundred, but not downhearted at all. I still had my "Victorian walnut work box" a very real treasure chest.

Chapter 26: Books

I only have to type the title of the most obscure reference work on antique silver into a search engine for every copy for sale across the globe to be lain before me. Why was it never this simple when I was a boy?

When you bought a book in my family it was only ever from W.H.Smith. Newsagent, stationer, toy shop, record store and yes, of course, book shop. The white metal and plastic bookshelves formed slanted rows sneaking into the very darkest corners at the back of the shop. The most popular titles and genres were well within easy reach of the tills, celebrity biographies bathed in window daylight, but it was quite a long gloomy walk, all the way back to the "antiques section". Calling it a section might have been overstating it at that. A bottom shelf and a half, hiding under more popular general and military histories. You got down on the floor to browse the antiques books, like every other part of the antiques world it brought you, quite literally, to your knees.

Imagine that you hadn't the first clue about antiques and had no one to tell you anything. It was a bit like learning a language everyone else was already speaking by having to speak it. Confusing, hard and strewn with pitfalls. The books that W.H.Smith stocked were "general publications" to put it kindly. Lyle and Millers price guides, antiques "picture books" those were the mainstay. Then perhaps an "encyclopaedia" of antiques, cobbled together by the good, the bad and the very bad and, possibly because it was always small and cheap, a pocket guide of hallmarks. I wasn't clever or discerning, I didn't have that luxury so I bought, over time and as pocket money allowed, almost all of them.

Bit by bit I learnt, in the words of Obi-Wan-Kenobi, that "these were not the books I was looking for". Odd second hand titles at village hall fairs and latterly the arrival of the discount bookshop furnished me the better reading. The discount bookshop was best. Arcane, obscure and really quite academic volumes which had no business appearing in a Birmingham shopping centre were remaindered for a pound or two. My first detailed book on Japanese lacquer came from there, a good one for all of three British pounds, though the cover price was fifty. Each good book was like a shaft of light breaking into the ignorant dark, illuminating me a little bit more. In antiques it works like this, the more you learn the further you realise you have to go. You never, ever arrive but at least you know you're on the right path.

Steadily the house was filling up with books, magazines and articles. Every little scrap on something else, something new, pointing the way to another even more obscure title which you had to get, though some of those proved almost unattainable in the getting.

Before the online search existed any slightly obscure publication could prove a holy grail of sorts. I could weep now at how long it took to find a copy of Martin Gubbins thin blue paperback book on York silver. Four pounds ninety five pence when published yet my first copy cost forty pounds and took a couple of years searching and asking everyone I knew to find. Other books were even harder, though the hardest were those you still didn't know existed.

The good books, the best books, I gradually realised, were those that HAD to be written. That is to say that the person writing them had researched a subject for so long and so thoroughly (usually born out of the passion that is collecting) that all these facts and insights reached a critical mass. All the knowledge had nowhere else to go but "out" and inevitably at some point breeched into a fully formed tome.

Unexpectedly but possibly inevitably my turn came when a decade of looking, researching and writing short articles built up to the need to put it all down in one place. Gubbins was always going to be the foundation, the immovable bedrock, but there were running repairs and a little more on top to build. That's how I came about visiting the Ledger.

Only one official piece of archival material on York silver was known, the Assay Office Ledger for 1805-21. It was referenced in Martin Gubbin's seminal work on York silver but I'd never seen it. I determined to do as complete a work as I possibly could and obtained permission not only to photograph the Ledger in its entirety but to publish a transcription of it when I was done.

Mum drove me up to York one bitter winter's morning as I nervously and excitedly fiddled with two digital cameras (belt and braces) and a couple of note books, getting everything in order. I'd practiced photographing some old documents at home the week earlier and was pretty sure I could get useable images on the day, at least I hoped I could.

We arrived with considerable intention through one of City's ancient stone gates, negotiating uneven Medieval cobbled streets and settled into the warm of the Library for several hours. Mum was bored rigid bless her as she quietly looked on at me taking multiple images of each of the 176 pages of text, carefully turning each page, smoothing it flat, lining it up. After three or four images I'd pause and check each one was clear and still legible when enlarged and then methodically continued on to the next page, then the next, then the next. I was beginning to get a better understanding of the meaning of the word "laborious". Eventually it was done and I thanked the Librarian for the permissions and said I'd let them know how it was all going. As we drove back home I think I might have thought, just for a moment, that the hard work was behind me, but I'd have been a fool if I did.

A week later and all I'd done was upload and tidy up the images of the Ledger. Then a message arrived from the Librarian that they had received another inquiry regarding possibly copying the Ledger and wanted to know how it was going? A starting pistol had been fired and from that moment on it was a race to the finish, but this was not going to be a sprint, this was a marathon…or two.

Each day was like the next now. I'd wake and dress (six or seven) and immediately start up the computer. Transcribing, by hand, each page of the Ledger into a hardback A4 ruled notebook purchased specifically for the purpose. Days turned quickly to weeks before just a third of it was done. I stopped, or more correctly was stopped, only by Mum calling me down for meals at regular intervals, a few of which were even refused. I was making real progress until the morning I spotted a small error, or rather finally got my eye properly into the manner of the writing of the text. There had been a small squiggle after some entries beside quantities of items. I'd taken it initially as an "etc" abbreviation, but after staring at page after page I began to realise it was a drunken ampersand with a hastily scribbled number after it. It could be "&4" or "&7" but it did mean, now that I could understand it, going back to the very beginning of the Ledger and amending the hundreds of small notations already made, more days passed.

Six or seven weeks saw the triumphant finish of this hand written transcript. All (did I say all?), well all that remained was finding a way to publish it. A friend had already told me that a small book he'd written had cost him about £15,000 to publish! This was using the services of designers, publishers, proof readers etc, etc. This was completely out of the question for me, money was almost non existent and I hadn't been working whilst writing. If it was going to be done, ridiculous as the idea might be, I was going to have to do every required process myself.

I found some publishing software (pretty basic) for £25 and loaded it up onto the computer. After a couple of days messing around I found it simple and easy to use so drew up a template for the Ledger pages and began typing up my hand written copy. It took a while, though I quickly learnt to regularly back-up work already done, when a finger slipped and two unexpectedly deleted pages of work caused me to swear, non stop, for about half an hour. "Digitising" it all took as long again, quicker in that I knew what the text actually was, but slower in that I had to type it, "idiot two finger typing" at its best.

Months had passed by the time I'd finished. I'd also catalogued and photographed items, composed complete tables of marks, all broken down into sections, made notes for the individual items and most importantly had my transcription of the Ledger all done. An enormous feeling of relief fell over me knowing it was finished. Though that didn't last very long.

The Ledger was transcribed, saved as a faithful copy should anything happen to the original, but what actual use was it? I had intended it be a reference for anyone who needed it, but how useful could it be if you need to scour all of its 176 pages each time you wanted to look something up? It was a Ledger in desperate need of an index. Okay I thought, that's not a problem, I'll just write an index for it. The index, it transpired, would take longer than the transcription had and it would have been near on impossible without the use of the computer.

I picked through each entry. Noting the maker with a letter code for ease of use and the quantity of each item whenever it was more than one. Each new object required a bold title, each new entry had to be slotted after the last, all in order, all in different sections of an ever expanding index list. As the list grew so did the time it took to scroll up and down to find the right entry. What took seconds at first could take a minute and with thousands of entries to make and double check, minutes became hours, days, then weeks.

I forget now quite how long it took, all I can say is it took months filled only with days when I did nothing but work on the book. The last little bit to do after contacting the printer was finally designing a cover.

Years and years earlier that impish scholar of Indian Colonial silver had found a small vibrant green trade card for one of the York Silversmiths. He'd put it aside for me and when I went to pay and pick it up he said, off hand, "this would make a nice cover for a book on York silver I you ever wrote one". Did he know even back then that I might? Did he put the idea in my head for it to pop out a decade later, who knows, but I'd like to thank him if he did. The cover of the book clearly had to be that very trade card and then it was all done, finished at last. I had to add corrections after it was published, my proof reading fell a little short. But every single part of it, every inch was my own work, good or bad. Only 100 copies were ever (and will ever) be printed and they now reside in such far flung places as Australia, Canada and America. I remember my sister's surprise and her very words upon being given one of the first copies: "I know you said it was a book, but it's a book, a REAL book" Believe me, praise doesn't get much better than this.

Even I couldn't quite believe it, perhaps I still can't, opening up the first box of books and holding the very first copy in my hands. That it existed seemed unreal, but the work, the near endless work it took to bring it to that point paled into insignificance against the joy of physically holding it, opening it up, ruffling through the pages. If I did nothing else with my life I had done this.

Some time later the author of one of those childhood W.H.Smith Antiques guides that had been my first port of call all those many years ago got in contact with me, completely out of the blue. It transpired that, alongside another expert they were jointly publishing a book and would very much like me to assist with a chapter or two. The book was to be the "standout work in its field" and they had asked if I would contribute to edit a section but also include all the photographs and details from my own book on York Silver and provide copyright. There would, they said, sadly be no remuneration for this as "budgets were tight" BUT I would have the honour and privilege of being associated with their publication. Hmmm.

This is how a mugging should be done in a civilised society. You shouldn't simply leap up behind someone and kosh them over the back of the head, stealing their wallet, keys and phone. No, you should politely inform them that being robbed by them was a certain privilege offered to a select few and if you wanted that honour you could simply send them your wallet, keys and phone by return of post. They'd then be happy to write your name down on a list of people they had robbed.

I declined their kind offer.

A week passed and I received a further entreaty from them, this time accompanied by a rough draft of a chapter introduction. They were nothing if not persistent. They could, they found, offer a small cash remuneration for my services after all, but they would need all my images, permission for worldwide copyright and for me to write the entire section of the book. The remuneration could not be large as "they were probably going to lose money publishing the book", but it was a token of their goodwill.

The offer then was this, that they should still mug me, taking my wallet, keys and phone BUT with the important difference that once they'd mugged me they would open my wallet and give me a few pence back. How I didn't swear in my reply I don't know, I think the outrageous and ridiculous nature of the request, the bare faced cheek of it, took any real venom out of the situation. This had all the sophistication of attempting to rob a Bank dressed as clowns armed only with custard pies and telling the Police beforehand about the robbery.

Unsurprisingly their book was published without my involvement. To this day I have never seen a copy other than those few draft pages that they sent, which had more factual inaccuracies in them than a Swiss cheese has holes. I've asked friends if I could look at their copies out of morbid curiosity but it turns out that none of them have bought it. Confirming I have very good taste in friends. Still the profit margins may not have been as slender as the author/publishers first made out to me with copies cheaply printed & shipped in from China (as many such publications are) first selling for £125 each, though a few years and honest online reviews later that has now been "somewhat reduced" to £21 on some well known websites. The back cover, I'm told, features large images of both "authors" (the word used in its loosest sense) with big biographies exclaiming their expertise upon a subject they mostly asked other people to write about.

Despite the odd bad apple, books are the foundation and GOOD books are the very roots that feed our world of antiques and we must never forget the debt we owe to those that sweat blood and tears (and the odd brain cell) to write them.

If I count on the fingers of my hands, including thumbs and name just Grimwade, Morgan, Culme, Gill, Gubbins, Kent, Jackson, Dove, Wilkinson and Ridgway. Just these, these few books. Take them away then we're all back to the Stone Age, scratching our heads in ignorance again. These are the good books, the books written out of a passion for a subject and with half a lifetime's knowledge. I honestly don't think any one of those authors ever made more than the price of a good dinner out of writing their books (I certainly didn't) but they stand up now as testament, pillars on which we can stand to reach a little higher.

But do beware and remember that for every good book sadly there is a bad one, hastily thrown together just to make money out of you. They are usually bright, glossy and often have someone's smiling photograph plastered all over them. They're probably smiling, grinning, leering because they neither had to read nor write the book, with their picture on the cover, that they hope you are about to buy.

Chapter 27: Patience

It was just after opening, always the best time to view a sale.

Early in the morning, especially if it's still a couple of days away from the actual auction, it's quietest then, leaving you unimpeded and hopefully not overlooked by any other prospective bidder. I can't recall precisely why I'd gone to view in person (the internet was in full flow) though it was a saleroom that wasn't too far away from home, a nice easy drive and there was lots of parking provided when you arrived. So perhaps it was just that I fancied a day out, though it was going to prove to be a day to be remembered.

Bags of miscellaneous flatware were passed back and forth from the cabinets by the porter at a speed he clearly weren't used to. I didn't hang around. Tipping each sealed plastic bag open on the counter and very quickly (as is my way) sifting through every spoon, knife and fork to hopefully elicit a single treasure that had been overlooked by the cataloguer. That day none were to be found. About a hundred and fifty lots in total were in the sale. Unspectacular cream jugs, sauceboats, tea sets and coffee pots. Odd little boxes, dressing table sets, but nothing really special or rare, nothing to get the juices flowing. Which was probably just as well, I didn't have the money for a real treasure.

Just before finishing up and going to leave I noticed two knife boxes at the bottom of one of the silver cabinets. Quite dark and filthy dirty, at first I thought they were overspill from the furniture and works of art being sold on the same day, but no, these were clearly part of the silver. No harm, I thought, in taking a look before I left.

If you're unfamiliar with them, knife boxes appeared during the 17th century (a rare few earlier), most commonly taking the form of a hinged, slant lidded, rectangular upright box which contained individual internal divisions to accommodate a single knife, fork or spoon, usually in graduated rows. At the beginning of the 18th century they became bow fronted, with carrying handles and escutcheon lock plates, either veneered in fine figured woods, tooled gilt leather or covered in a protective layer of robust shagreen (treated ray or shark skin). Both of the ones before me were in black shagreen, an early feature but less sought after than the slightly later, prettier, polished green examples. The metal mounts were in brass, not silver and neither had supporting feet, so my hopes were not high, even though both boxes were estimated at a hefty thousand pounds each.

True to form the first one was exactly and disappointingly what I expected it would be. It had a rather tatty felt interior with bits missing or worn. It was fully fitted with Georgian silver handled knives and forks, but as with all these sets they had been well used. The handles were ubiquitous stamped sheet silver, two matching halves soldered together and then filled with pitch, to give them strength but also fix the steel blade or prongs into the handle by means of a protruding tang.

Polishing these over the years, the centuries, causes them to "hole" on the highest parts of the decoration. Also the pitch becomes worn and brittle allowing the handles to dent or break. This set wasn't awful by any means, most of the pieces were ok, but a few had suffered from vigorous and particular use. A Great Aunt with a penchant for hefty amounts of corrosive marmalade on her muffins perhaps? Still I was sure they'd sell. Complete sets (which hadn't just been made up in the trade out of oddments) were, even then, becoming uncommon. Particularly as 99% of knife boxes, having been long redundant, had already in the late nineteenth century been converted into desk top letter or stationary boxes.

The second knife box, I was told by the lingering

porter as he handed up to me, was "from the same family" so my expectations for it were much the same. I was of course quite wrong.

With just the two of us in the saleroom I could let an unguarded look of wonder flood over my face as I lifted the hinged lid of this second knife box, just as Indiana Jones had lifted the lid off the Ark of the Covenant. The velvet lining was all original, bright burgundy velvet, not the muddy green of most. Each division was finely edged in pure silver brocade, some of which was a little frayed but still all there, as were the set of twelve knives and forks which each rectangular aperture accommodated.

Unlike the previous set these were earlier, about thirty years earlier and whilst you might not think that made much of a difference it absolutely did. Rather than being a simple pistol handle these were octagonal pistol handles (much rarer) but most of all these handles had been cast.

Casting a two piece handle required a great deal more silver to be used than stamping from a sheet, it was the most expensive way to do it. Thick heavy silver handles which would never "hole" or badly dent like their later counterparts. The whole set lay gleaming in the case. Each piece clearly stamped for the higher Britannia standard of silver, each with a makers mark, each with a superb and finely engraved crest. This was the holy grail of knife boxes and whilst it's counterpart was reckoned to be of similar value they were miles, leagues, galaxies apart. I would have been ecstatic but for one small thing, I simply could not afford to buy it.

Returning home I was delighted to have seen and handled such a wonderful set but, as was often the way, completely gutted at not being able to buy it. Later that day I was talking to Gerry (my old client, now firm friend) and the subject fell onto upcoming auctions and if I had seen anything nice? Was I being pumped for information? Certainly. Did I mind? No, not really. My attitude has always rather been to be less "secret squirrel" about things than most of the older trade, who would only tell you what day of the week it was if you held a calendar in front them and only then with a loaded gun to their head.

I spilled the beans about the fabulous knife box I'd just seen and how utterly wonderful it was. Enthusiasm is, when genuine, infectious and by the time I had hung up, Gerry, an older man of not inconsiderable means, was himself set upon its purchase. The sale was two days later and he had already booked a phone to bid.

As expected the first knife box which I'd quickly

dismissed came and went under the auctioneer's hammer in the briefest of disappointing moments, not quite making its thousand pound estimate and scraping away at nine hundred. There was profit in it for sure, but also a bit of work from a skilled hammer and soldering iron, no it made enough. The second knife box, the one I dearly wished I could buy was a different kettle of fish. Without betraying too many confidences that galloped away, bids flew in and thousands began to rapidly multiply. Gerry bought it and was perhaps a little shaken when he did given the sums involved. My hearty, though envy edged, congratulations on his purchase quickly assured him of the wisdom of his buy but could I also do him a favour? As it wasn't too far away from me could I go and pick it up? It may have been a test too far for friendships sake but I would at least get to see the set again before it found its new home. I gave my forelock a good hard tug and duly obliged.

When I'd got it back home I couldn't resist sitting and looking at the knife box and it's peerless contents. I doubt it had ever been used. All the steel blades and tines were the originals by Ephraim How of London (the leading cutler of his age) and the brass handles of the shagreen case were oxidised black, they had never I think seen a touch of polish. Mum was both observant and piteous in her summation of the whole affair, "you love these don't you?" She knew me too well.

Love's a strong word to use between a man and a knife box but if ever there was an occasion to use it, this was probably it. But love stories as we know seldom have happy endings so a day or so later the set was with its new owner and I was left a little, just a little, bereft.

After that almost every time I would speak to Gerry the knife box would crop up in the conversation. Every couple of years, finances allowing, I would make a run at it.

"Gerry, don't you want to sell that old knife box?"

I would slip in to the conversation when he least expected it but a hard refusal came back each time. It became a thing of myth and legend, it became "THE" knife box, as though no other existed on Earth.

Diligence, Kindness, Humility they are just three of the Cardinal Virtues. It was Diligence that found the knife box in the first place and then Kindness that told Gerry about it and a touch (just a touch) of Humility, when losing out myself I went to collect it for him. Of course these are not the only Cardinal Virtues.

Patience is a virtue too, my Nan told me that when I was little. Yes you must never forget Patience is a virtue.

Years had passed and Gerry had set his sights on his own white whale, though I advised him it would involve spending a LOT of money at auction which he wasn't too keen on, honestly who is? My advice to him was to sell odds and ends first. Pieces he bought very early on which simply weren't that great and would offset the cost of this potential new purchase, even outlining things that needed to go, though never for a second considering the knife box of legend. Then, out of the blue, it happened.

"Well what about that knife box, what would you give me for that?"

I'd just lost Mum and had been getting rid of everything I owned, so for the briefest of moments I actually could make him a serious offer, a decent turn more than he had paid in the first place, though of course I expected to be rebuffed.

"Sold!" came back his immediate reply, it happened as quickly as that. If I were overly sentimental I would say Mum even had a hand in it but it was all much simpler than that, it was as simple as Patience, which certainly is a Virtue.

Chapter 28: Death Bed

Once, years ago, an antiques fair tried to kill me.

Well, that's not entirely true. The fair didn't become sentient and immediately develop a conscious will to cause me mortal harm. It was an incidental side effect of having to queue outside for half an hour, on a very wet Sunday morning with friends, to get in to the fair. Young and foolish I had attended without an umbrella, a coat or even a carrier bag to place over my head as other dealers were doing. I simply got soaked and then dried off running around the stalls for the next couple of hours without a second thought. On balance a huge mistake, but I felt fine. The day after however I began to develop a "cold" of hitherto unimagined proportions, shivers, snot and silence ensued as I completely lost my voice for six weeks.

I eventually recovered but my defences had been irrevocably breached by that Sunday morning soaking. With a Breguet like precision, from then on, at exactly that time of year, no matter what precautions were taken, I'd be laid low with a "cold" which was anything but. Still I always got over it, eventually.

One year it came again but proved harder than usual to shake. I was reconciled to a long drawn out recovery but I must have looked a lot worse than I felt as a Doctor was called to the house. Remarkably the Doctor actually came within half an hour, surely some sort of record in the NHS. After a few minutes of light conversation and the delicate fingertip placement of a Oximeter, the Physician's brow began to furrow.

"I'd like you to go to hospital"

I looked over at my Mum and replied:

"Well, if you think it's really necessary Mum can drop me off a bit later this afternoon"

"No, now" came the reply, "I'll call an ambulance"

I wasn't singing or dancing at that point but I didn't feel any worse than I had with the colds from previous years. But the call had been made and just a few minutes later I was in my own episode of Casualty, stretchered into the hospital by two jolly (too jolly) paramedics, straight into a hospital bed. I was hooked up to a drip, a monitor and didn't feel that bad at all, except for concerns about the polite execution of one's toilet. It was a new ward, quiet and everything was "neatly to hand" so to speak. I was just appalled at the lack of a television.

For two days I lay there wondering if they'd let me out as quickly as they'd pulled me in, only to be told I was being moved to my own room. Was my general discourse with the other patients that unbearable I had to be siphoned off, away, to solitary confinement, possibly yes but that was not the reason.

"You may have the first case of swine flu this year in the country"

How very dare they, were they taking (in a non diagnostic fashion) the piss? Still I was immediately moved and although in a room of my own the facilities were to prove quite "basic".

"The loo?" I asked.

"It's just across the hall" the brusk, slightly muscular nurse replied. Pointing through my open door to another opposite the hallway.

"But the doctor has said you mustn't use it. You may be highly infectious so please use these."

She pointed to some bare worn metal and plastic utensils which were both Heath Robinson in their "unrelenting" construction with just a splash of the Marquis de Sade thrown in for good measure (splash being the operative word).

I nodded in gentle smiling compliance to her request, already full determined to use the facilities opposite as the need arose and when nobody was looking.

Hours passed and I was checked on every now and then (but not often), sleeping quite a bit and feeling tired. Eventually though the need "to go" arose and I was not prepared to piss in a cardboard bottle when a perfectly serviceable facility with somewhere to wash my hands was only a few steps away.

It must have been night by then, it was dark and the corridor lights were on, no one seemed to be around. I crept to the door and peeped round, then quietly, in stockinged feet, shuffled across to the WC unseen. Had this been a military raid in a fuel depot during World War II it couldn't have been going better, I was completely incognito, unnoticed and unobserved.

A quiet flush and wash saw me begin to totter back to my room only a few short feet away. It was then I began to realise I may not have been that well after all. I half turned and stretched out an arm to a distant nurse along the corridor. It was then, I think, that I began to fall, I don't remember anything else.

It's was several hours later that I was conscious again. I was fitted with an oxygen mask, stripped naked (under a sheet for modesty's sake) and had tubes, several thick tubes in various parts of me. Arms, necks, sides and unmentionables, some of which had been stitched in place so I wouldn't thrash and pull them out, some I could see, most were thankfully out of view.

I was now in intensive care with round the clock treatment. The first doctor I saw didn't tell me anything and tried not to look as worried as he was. He was at pains to say "don't worry about anything you said when you were delirious" not that I knew I had been.

"People say all sorts, don't give it a second thought". I professed I had no recollection past the visit to the toilet and waking up in ITU.

"Even better, nothing to worry about".

It was only later from a nurse who had been one of the seven people fighting hard to save my life that night (she told me with relish that "no one thought you were going to make it you know") that I had been calling both for a hotline to the Prime Minister and screaming for the immediate execution of the patient being treated, within earshot, in the opposite cubicle, whose name I must have overheard whilst in my delerium. Something which, on reflection, cannot have made his own treatment go as smoothly as it might, apologies.

I nodded off again, none the wiser and awoke now to a junior doctor at my bedside with one of the nurses looking earnestly on as they might do in Doctor Kildare. Unlike the more bombastic consultant I'd seen when first admitted her tone was more serious, quieter and more deliberate. I began to worry.

"Hello Mr Baggott, Michael, may I call you Michael?"

I managed a half smiling "Yes"

"I wondered if I could have a quiet word for a moment." The mood became serious. "I'd like to show you something"

Was this going to be it, a chart, doom laden with dropping pressures and unfortunate outcomes? Too soon, I thought, too soon. She reached down into her bag.

"I bought this at the weekend in a local charity shop. It was £5 and wondered if you could tell me about it?"

Lying naked, unwashed and bewildered under a thin sheet, urine siphoning off down one tube, six others pumping voluminous quantities of medicaments and nutrients to various parts of my anatomy, I reached up to clasp a small moulded glass preserve pot in the form of an apple out of the waiting, expectant junior doctor's hands.

"It's got a silver cover" I replied, "with a small cut out for the preserve ladle and is marked to the edge for sterling silver, James Dixon and sons assayed in Birmingham, 1937. It's worth about £30-50 as it stands".

She was delighted, beaming, saying:

"Thankyou very much, that was a fiver well spent"

taking the preserve pot back, wrapping it up and quickly leaving the room as she did so.

Startled, dumbfounded but highly amused I then knew I was over the worst of it. Antiques weren't going to let me get away that lightly.

Not to spoil the story but I then, much to the chagrin of many a dealer since and as you may have guessed, lived.

Antiques had put me in jeopardy of my life but in equal measure they had pulled free of it. Has another valuation ever been conducted not only in a hospital ITU but by the patient in one of its beds? Antiques take no prisoners, take no heed of circumstance, but they are a constant to which I've tied my star and so far they've never let me down, not even when I was briefly lying on my death bed.